THE MARIEL EXODUS: TWENTY YEARS LATER

A Study on the Politics of Stigma and a Research Bibliography

COLECCIÓN CUBA Y SUS JUECES

EDICIONES UNIVERSAL, Miami, Florida, 2002

GASTÓN A. FERNÁNDEZ

THE MARIEL EXODUS: TWENTY YEARS LATER

A Study on the Politics of Stigma and a Research Bibliography

EDICIONES UNIVERSAL

Primera edición, 2002

EDICIONES UNIVERSAL
P.O. Box 450353 (Shenandoah Station)
Miami, FL 33245-0353. USA
Tel: (305) 642-3234   Fax: (305) 642-7978
e-mail: ediciones@ediciones.com
http://www.ediciones.com

Library of Congress Catalog Card No.: 2002106640
I.S.B.N.: 0-89729-821-7

Composición de textos: Chemical Graphics
Diseño de la cubierta: Luis García Fresquet

To my parents for all their love and support

TABLE OF CONTENTS

About the Author

Dr. Gastón A. Fernández is Associate Professor of the Department of Political Science at Indiana State University, Terre Haute (ISU). He currently serves as the Executive Director of the International Affairs Center at ISU.

Dr. Fernández is the co-author of *Hispanic Migration to the United States* and has published numerous articles and invited book reviews on the topic of Cuban and Hispanic migration to the U.S. and Central America in *Cuban Studies/Estudios Cubanos*, in the *Journal of Inter-American Affairs*, and in the *International Migration Review*. He is a regular reviewer of manuscripts for the journal *International Migration Review*.

Dr. Fernández completed his Masters and Ph.D. degrees at the University of Wisconsin-Madison in Political Science and his undergraduate degree at the University of Arkansas-Fayetteville in Political Science. He has served on the executive board of various Latin American Studies and International studies associations including the Indiana Consortium for International Programs, Institute of Cuban Studies and the Midwest Latin American Studies Association.

Preface

The Mariel exodus and its aftermath represent one of the most controversial and tragic episodes in the history of migrations to the United States. The Mariel Cubans as a group became the target of a sustained Cuban regime policy to stigmatize the migrants as delinquents and criminals, and the U.S. press and much of public opinion accepted and magnified many of the negative stereotypes about the migrants.

Research on the migrants since 1980 suggests that for a large number of the Mariel Cubans the American dream remains elusive. Despite the many contributions of Mariel Cubans to the economy, culture and the arts- for many adjustment to the U.S. has remained elusive. For others, their experience with the U.S. government has been one of a sustained policy of persecution and detention by the criminal justice system. This study seeks to provide a comprehensive guide to the research on the experiences of this group and to suggest an expanded perspective on this complex topic.

Part I of this study analyzes the political factors behind the origins and perpetuation of the Mariel stigma. It reviews the scholarly literature on the Mariel migration beginning with the research on the background characteristics of the group placing this migration in the context of the larger Cuban migration to the U.S. It examines the processes by which the Mariel stigma originated inside Cuba and how it transferred to the U.S. where it was amplified and sustained. This part contributes to the understanding of this phenomenon of stigmatization by an in-depth analysis of the role of internment at Ft. Chaffee, Arkansas. The experience at Chaffee provides a microcosm of how the Mariel stereotype played out in American policy-making towards the migrants.

Part II consists of a research bibliography on the Mariel migration. I have divided the literature into categories building on earlier bibliographic studies by Boswell et. al. and Fernández-Narvaez. The categories used in this study expand and update the previous focus on demographic backgrounds, camp experiences, adaptation experiences and so forth to include topics such as experiences with the U.S. criminal system.

Part II divides the literature on Mariel into categories including books, book chapters, academic journal articles (general social sciences and law journals), dissertations and thesis, government documents, newspaper articles and internment camp publications from 1980-2000. A special emphasis is placed on materials related to the Chaffee experience, which provides a context for understanding the analysis in Part I. Since there is a considerable body of literature on Cuban immigration, this bibliography tries to focus specifically on the Mariel experience, and therefore, items included deal with aspects of their experience as more than a passing reference. This section provides a topical index for future research on the topic of the Mariel migration, which I hope will facilitate the future work of scholars by providing a quick reference to particular topics of interest. Some items are cross-referenced.

Dr. Gastón A. Fernández
Indiana State University
January 2002

Acknowledgements

This manuscript would not have been completed without the assistance and support of many to whom I am deeply thankful. I benefited enormously in the compilation of the bibliographic materials from the assistance provided to me by dedicated research librarians specializing in Latin America and the Caribbean at the University of Arkansas, Fayetteville, the Carter Library in Atlanta, the University of Wisconsin Madison and the Cuban Special Collection at the University of Miami, Florida.

I especially want to acknowledge the assistance provided to me by Mr. John Harrison, Director of Libraries at the University of Arkansas, for extending his support during the time I spent researching the special collection. I also extend my thanks to Mr. Stephen Perry, Librarian and Latin American specialist at the University of Arkansas-Fayetteville. Mr. Perry was most generous with his time and knowledge of the Collection in assisting me in the compilation of the materials at the University of Arkansas.

I am also indebted to Dr. Esperanza de Varona, Director of the Cuban Special Collections at the University of Miami, Florida, for her assistance in this project. The Special Collections was most generous in providing me with access to the materials in the Collection.

I especially thank my father, Dr. Gastón F. Fernández de la Torriente, who is a deeply committed scholar of Cuban affairs, and who read and commented on many drafts of this manuscript. His comments and suggestions on this project were greatly appreciated and challenged me to examine many of my assumptions about how to best categorize the body of literature presented in this manuscript. He also provided invaluable assistance and advice in the compilation of the materials included in this research bibliography. My mother, Catalina Fernández' skills as a Librarian and her unwavering support for this project both greatly contributed to the project's final completion. I greatly appreciated the time she spent in Indiana helping with the grandchildren while I was conducting the research project.

I also want to thank Dean Joe Weixlmann, College of Arts and Sciences, Indiana State University, for his support for a sabbatical leave from the College. The leave provided me with the needed time to carry out the research for the manuscript. His support and encouragement are greatly appreciated.

Mr. Eduardo Conde, himself a Mariel Cuban, provided me with much logistical support in conducting this research while in Fayetteville, Arkansas.

Finally, I want to thank Linda Fernández for her patience during the project, and for her encouragement. Both are greatly appreciated.

All errors and omissions in the manuscript are my own.

The Mariel Exodus:
Twenty Years Later

Introduction

Why this study of Mariel now? It is appropriate to assess the Mariel migratory experience as at the twenty-year mark since their first arrival in the U.S. The Marielitos have contributed greatly to the cultural and economic development of South Florida. Their contributions extend to the arts, literature and entrepreneurial successes. Yet, despite their many accomplishments, the fact remains that, as a group, they have experienced higher socio-economic marginality and higher rates of incarceration in the U.S. than previous waves of migrants. Research on Mariel is sufficiently robust to allow for a more comprehensive evaluation of their experience after two decades in the U.S. and to assess the extent to which they were really "different."

Prior to 1980, Cuban migrants were variously termed as "worms" and "traitors" in official Cuban political discourse and as "refugees" and "freedom-loving" exiles in the U.S. This changed in 1980, to a stereotype of the immigrants as "undesirable" and "threats" to both societies. The Marielitos' resettlement experience, especially of detainees at Ft. Chaffee was an especially significant episode in this transformation. For a large number of the so-called Mariel Cubans (approximately 20% of all the Cubans leaving through Mariel harbor spent time at the camp) Chaffee was a significant part of their initiation to the U.S. Fort Chaffee played a crucial role in the metamorphosis of the Cuban immigrant from refugee to undesirable. The camp became a national symbol of the Cubans' marginal status and, therefore, illuminates the processes by which changes in the construction of this group's identity occured. This study sheds light on this social transformation, especially focusing on the Marielitos experiences at Ft. Chaffee, which became a national symbol for the "pathological" stigma of the immigrants.

A Brief Background to Cuban Migration

Recent Cuban migrations to the U.S. were in response to the Cuban revolution of 1959. Beginning in 1959, after the flight of "Batistianos" following the revolution, the exodus gained force with Cuba's nationalization of industries and banks in the summer and fall of 1960. President Dwight Eisenhower responded to the influx by establishing the Cuban Refugee Emergency Center, known as the "Refugio" to assist the émigrés with resettlement. The President funded the program with $1 million in discretionary funds to assist the émigrés in finding jobs and with initial relief. In February of 1961, President Kennedy established the Cuban Refugee Assistance Program (CRP) with an initial funding allocation of $4 million.

The CRP had expanded authority to establish cooperation between federal and state agencies and private voluntary resettlement agencies. This program received permanent legal authority under the Migration and Refugee Assistance Act of 1962. The Act provided the legal basis for the liberal admissions policy for Cubans under which hundreds of thousands of Cuban émigrés entered the U.S. in the two decades before Mariel, and were given asylum and the opportunity to become permanent legal residents and citizens. Under its authority, the Cuban Refugee Assistance Program (CRP) was expanded, providing Cuban émigrés close to a billion dollars from 1962-80 in various forms of assistance including cash assistance, health and education assistance, special employment training and related services, and resettlement assistance.

Under President Lyndon Johnson, Public Law 89-732, enacted in 1966, provided those arriving directly from Cuba with the opportunity to become legal residents without the expensive requirement of applying for permanent residency at a U.S. Consulate abroad. The Act responded to the large number of illegal crossings following the October Missile Crisis of 1962. Between 1962 and 1965, nearly 30,000 émigrés arrived in the U.S. illegally, about 5,000 via an illegal boatlift from the Port of Camarioca resembling the Mariel exodus.The 1966 Act permitted the Attorney General to adjust the status of any Cuban national to permanent resident alien if physically present in the U.S. for at least two years. Mariel refugees were aware of the importance of this law as a gateway to U.S. society.

The U.S. allowed entry to more than 750,000 Cubans between 1960-76. Cubans of all backgrounds undertook the journey to America, although immigrant waves significantly differed in the migrants' social background. The first migration wave between 1959-62 represented primarily the elites: sugar mill owners, ranchers, executives and upper middle class professionals; more than 153,000 émigrés made up this first wave. From October 1962 - November 1965, nearly 30,000 émigrés of different backgrounds, mostly middle class, arrived. President Johnson's agreement with Cuba to establish "freedom flights" to stem the illegal flow of émigrés brought an additional 264,000 émigrés largely small merchants, independent craftsmen, and skilled and unskilled workers between 1965 and 1973.[1]

The Mariel Migration

On April 1, a small group of would-be refugees seeking asylum crashed a bus into the gates of the Peruvian Embassy in Havana killing a Cuban guard. The Peruvian's refusal to turn over the Cubans led an angry Fidel Castro to withdraw Cuban guards from outside the embassy expecting that a few troublemakers would crowd into the Embassy embarrassing the Peruvians. By April 6, over 10,800 Cubans had entered the Embassy's grounds.

Studies of the exodus highlight several factors as contributing significantly to the Mariel migration. The Cuban economy was experiencing strains related to crop blights that severely damaged major sugar and tobacco export crops. The resulting crisis aggravated social and economic conditions and led to shortages in medicines, food and other basic inputs such as oil. One manifestation of this crisis was the growth in unemployment, especially among younger workers.[2]

The downturn was exacerbated by the Cuban government's decision in December of 1978 to allow Cuban-Americans to visit the Island.[3] This decision followed increased cultural exchanges with Cuba during the Carter administration including the commencement of commercial flights between Miami and Havana and the granting of short-term visitors visas to Cubans to the U.S. Numerous Cuban artists, scientists, scholars visited the U.S. during the months preceding the Mariel migration. The freeing of travel restriction for Cuban-Americans led to over 100,000 visitors traveling to Cuba, and spending over $100 million dollars throughout 1979 and early 1980. This stream of visitors precipitated the so-called "blue-jean revolution" (because the returning émigrés usually brought gifts such as designer jeans for their relatives) and a rise in expectations at a time when the Cuban economy was experiencing severe austerity.[4] Reported opportunities for advancement in the U.S. described by Cuban-American tourists encouraged emigration to the U.S. The "blue jean revolution" was a significant part of the environment facing the Cuban government in 1980, and it added a segment of younger émigrés seeking a better life to others seeking family unification and dissidents fleeing government persecution.

The Mariel wave of 124,700 Cubans arrived between April and October of 1980. Four groups of immigrants made up the Mariel wave: ex-political prisoners and other dissidents that were pressured to leave by government officials and members of the state-run Committees for the Defense of the Revolution; "several thousand social undesirables comprised of petty criminals, mentally disturbed persons, homosexuals (sic) and juvenile delinquents;" "antisocials" (a category which included religious evangelists such as Jehovah's Witnesses, alcoholics, prostitutes, vagrants charged under the "Dangerousness Law" of 1979); and individuals with family members already living in the U.S. who had an expressed desire to join them (by far the largest segment). This latter group's importance in the migration was underplayed by the media because they were less newsworthy.[5]

Mariel Cubans differed in several significant respects from the earlier migrations; there was a larger number of males (almost 70%) and a larger percentage of blacks or mulattoes (estimated at 25 - 40%). In socio-economic terms, the Mariel migrants resembled the social and economic diversity of Cuba and did not differ significantly from the 1970's arrivals. On balance, the migrants occupied a higher socioeconomic position than the average Cuban. *Table 1* summarizes the principal occupation of the immigrants processed through the resettlement camps.

TABLE 1

Principal Occupation in Cuba for Cuban Entrants at Each Resettlement Camp: Persons 16 Years of Age and Over (percents)

Occupation	Eglin	Chafee	Indiantown	McCoy	Total
Professional/ Technical	7.4	8.6	11.7	9.2	9.4
Administrator	1.3	2.1	2.7	2.1	2.1
Sales	1.3	1	2.1	0.5	1.3
Clerical	5.8	4.9	6.5	2.5	5
Craft	22.5	26.5	23.8	26.8	25.3
Operative	15.2	16	13.1	17.3	15.4
Transport Operative	10.8	10.9	11	10.7	11
Laborer	22.2	18.9	15.9	18.9	18.8
Farm Labor	1.1	1.8	1.8	3.4	2
Farmer	0.3	1.3	1.8	2.1	1.4
Service	97.2	100	100	99.9	100
Total	97.2	100	100	99.9	100

Robert Bach, Jennifer Bach and Timothy Triplett, "The Flotilla Entrants: Latest and Most Controversial," Cuban Studies/Estudios Cubanos. Vol. 11 No. 2 July 1981 and Vol. 12 No. 1 January 1982. p. 47.

The social composition of Mariel Cubans was strongly influenced by the political context. Despite the overwhelming evidence that this migration was shaped primarily by forces traditionally influencing Cuban out-migration (namely family

reunification and political prisoner/ dissident status in Cuba),
the focus on the small criminal element, a mentally "disturbed" population, and the younger, Afro-Cuban immigrants
led to the proliferation of new categories to classify these
migrants. Poorly defined categories (for example, "social undesirables" and "antisocial") reflected mass media and bureaucratic terminology used in the resettlement process to classify
Marielitos. The stigmatizing of the immigrants as undesirables
dominated the mass media' representation of the exodus.

The Experience with Departure in Cuba

The Cuban government's role in the migration involved
mobilizing resources to stereotype the Marielitos as pathological. The role of the state was dictated by domestic and international objectives pursued during the unfolding migration.
Domestically, the regime promoted the stigma of Mariel
pathology in order to appeal to loyalists and mobilize party
members, workers and the military behind the government.
Internationally, it sought to use the stigma as a "bullet" to
advance foreign policy goals.

The break-in into the Peruvian Embassy demonstrated the
regime's diminishing capacity to control its borders and the
dangers to the regime of continued loss of control over its
environment. Events during April 6 to 14 reinforced this perception. The numbers of would-be refugees at the Embassy
escalated to over 10,800. The departure of several hundreds
to Costa Rica and Panamá on April 14 proved an embarrassment. President Castro was particularly angered by Costa
Rican President Rodrigo Carazo personally welcoming the
first planeload of émigrés, and by Costa Rican plans to construct a high profile staging area in San Jose for the Cubans'
use prior to dispersal to countries of final destination. The
arrival in Costa Rica and Perú of the first 1,000 Cubans from
the Peruvian Embassy shouting "libertad" as they deplaned in
those countries reinforced the negative international consequences of the migration.

U.S. press coverage of the Peruvian Embassy also raised the
political stakes for Cuban authorities. The media portrayed
the break-in as evidence of the Cuban regime's failures. For

example, the *Chicago Tribune* on April 8 editorialized that "the incident should serve as a sobering lesson to those in Latin America and the Caribbean who look to Cuba as a model and mentor... if after two decades of communist rule, so many thousands are willing to take such a desperate gamble to flee their native land, obviously there is something terribly wrong with Castroism."[6]

The multilateral response to the Marielitos in the Peruvian Embassy crisis further embarrassed the Cuban government. The Peruvian government's call for support to relief effort from the Andean Pact countries - Bolivia, Colombia, Ecuador, Venezuela - and the commitments from the U.S., Costa Rica, Argentina, West Germany, France and Spain to accept immigrants effectively internationalized the crisis. It appeared that the exodus would be a large and orderly migration that would expedite the flow of Cubans to the U.S. and other nations and underscore the vulnerabilities of the Cuban regime.

The Cuban government changed direction in stereotyping the Marielitos after April 14. On April 17, Fidel Castro discontinued the Costa Rican flights insisting on direct flights from Havana to the country of settlement. This decision changed the focus of the migration and created diplomatic problems over the distribution of émigrés among hemisphere countries. On April 20, Castro reversed this stand and unilaterally announced that Cuba's Mariel port was open, rejecting all efforts to establish an orderly departure. Appeals from Great Britain and Costa Rica in early May, following the San José Conference were rejected as international meddling in Cuban affairs. President Carter's May 14 Five Point proposal for an orderly sea and air lift, permitting prior screening in Cuba, was also rebuffed by Castro a few days later.

The Origins of the Pathological Stigma

The Cuban government response to this political situation was to increasingly portray the émigrés as pathological. The Committees for the Defense of the Revolution were the principal instrument of state power in this process. Strategies for stigmatizing the deviance included coercing would-be refugees to collaborate with the official discourse, which labeled them

23

as "lumpens" as part of the cost to them of joining the exodus.[7] Would-be émigrés were required to surrender to authorities all official Cuban identity cards, passports and other materials which could identify them in the U.S. and were forced to obtain special "cartas de escoria."

The spectacle of public confessions of deviance and criminality validated official ideology, while reinforcing the status and power of party loyalists over the migration. Permission to migrate required confessions of illegal or undesirable behaviors in Cuba such as homosexuality, vandalizing property, and taking drugs. These acts had to be acknowledged and certified before local authorities of the Committees for the Defense of the Revolution (CDR) as illegal behavior under the Title XI of the Cuban Penal Code as "Acts of Dangerousness."[8] These bureaucratic processes were part of constructing a deviant social identity in Cuba. They also bred distrust and schisms among the Marielitos. Subsequently, the émigrés' willingness in the U.S. to use Cuban bureaucratic classifications as "antisocial" to demonstrate their opposition to the regime to U. S. officials, researchers, reporters and others abetted the transfer of negative images of the émigrés to the U.S.

The regime's response to the exodus involved tapping nationalist sentiments and socialist ideology. Cuban officials who used the migrants as symbols of deviance included the top leadership in the Communist Party, the mass media, and the bureaucratic instruments of state power, especially the Committees for the Defense of the Revolution. Stereotyping involved recasting the conflict over emigration crisis in nationalistic terms familiar to Cubans. The tactical move gave to Cuban authorities control over the situation and helped transform the émigrés into a symbol of the Cuban government's power over its enemies. On May 4, GRANMA stressed this indicating that "Cuba will now have to be reckoned with" as regards to permits for Cubans admitted to the U.S.[9]

Once the struggle was recast as a U.S.-Cuban conflict, the stigma assigned to the would-be émigrés was linked to deeply ingrained national symbols of resistance to foreign aggression. The Cuban press played an important role in the political transformation of the Mariel émigrés. For example, a GRANMA cartoon published on April 27 shows the Peruvian

Embassy with Uncle Sam behind a trash can filled with a few cowering Cubans surrounded by a throng of people waiving banners proclaiming "another victory of Girón." It depicts the émigrés as a fifth column in a U.S. invasion similar to the Bay of Pigs. The cartoon thus evoked powerful national symbols of resistance to U.S. aggression and of Cuban political triumphs.This appeal to nationalist sentiments allowed the regime to mobilize mass organizations against the émigrés. The Playa Girón celebrations in April became a proxy for mass attacks on the would-be refugees in the Embassy compound, many of whom refused to leave the compound for fear of their lives.

The migrants were increasingly portrayed as a "solution" to achieve important regime goals. The Cuban press highlighted propaganda objectives, such as the Freedom Flotilla's circumventing de facto the embargo. President Castro also linked the migration to broader issues such as terminating the embargo and regulating emigration policy, turning the situation into political advantage. In this regard, the Mariel exodus became a tactical advantage to the Cuban government: to maximize the tactic, the regime needed to develop the émigré's identity as threats to the U.S. society. The regime largely succeeded in fostering the perception of the émigrés as "bullets" aimed at the U.S.

Fidel Castro's May Day rally speech drew the distinction between the Mariel émigrés and previous émigrés and the Cuban people. Addressing the issue of the émigrés' dissident labeling, he stated that "our enemies launched this international campaign with the idea that the people who wanted to leave... were dissidents. Some of the lumpen in that embassy as you can see... don't even understand what the word 'dissident' means." Castro portrayed the Mariel émigrés' difference from the earlier refugees by contrasting their social marginality with the political and economic basis of dissent of the earlier migrants composed of the "refined bourgeoisie" and "well-dressed landowners" followed by the "professionals." The Mariel émigrés, according to Castro, were "lumpen," defined as loafers, parasites, criminals and addicts."[10]

The émigrés were labeled deviants in terms of Cuban socialism, representing a different kind of threat not based on class differences and interests, but on character flaws and behaviors contributing to economic and social ills of Cuba. This characterization of the émigrés as deviants drew moral boundaries separating them from the regime's supporters while asserting the superiority of those outside the boundaries of Mariel. As Castro indicated, "we don't need those who don't have revolutionary genes, revolutionary blood, minds adapted to the idea of a revolution and hearts adapted to the efforts and heroism of a revolution."[11]

Domestically, Fidel Castro's 1980 speech at Las Tunas appealed to workers and soldiers by associating Cuban unemployment and low productivity problems with the lumpen element who take up good jobs but fail to contribute their share of the work. According to Fidel Castro, "We even have some unemployment problems. So sometimes, it is not easy to place into a basic industry an individual who has been demobilized from military service... If we have an unpatriotic individual, a weakling, who is holding a job and who wants to go to the Yankee paradise — good luck to him."

The construction of Marielitos as deviants served important regime goals. Domestically, the regime reassured its supporters that the migration represented the social cleansing of Cuba. Fidel Castro emphasized this to workers at the Las Tunas factory stating that "we also have our own delinquents (drug addicts, prostitutes, gamblers and all of that). Well, we used to. We have reduced those a bit... the housecleaning has been considerable, people of Las Tunas know this perfectly well."

The strategy of stigmatizing included directly releasing some émigrés from prison to form part of the exodus, although the exact numbers are not known. President Castro makes reference to this fact stating that some were "given the alternative of leaving prison, of being released and of traveling into Yankee paradise" or remaining in prison. In the same speech, he categorizes those who were given the option as being "thieves of chickens, sheep, hogs and other things," prostitutes, gamblers and drug users who are not considered as criminals in the U.S. The Cuban government emphasized that only petty criminals had the "choice" of leaving Cuba. According to the official line, those who were guilty of com-

26

mitting violent crimes, "deeds of blood," and the mentally ill were not "intentionally" included in the exodus.

The Infiltration of Criminal Elements and the Pathology Stereotype

No one knows for certain the exact number of prisoners and ex-prisoners included in the boatlift, although eyewitness reports and the Mariel refugees own statements confirm that hardened criminals were forced to join the boatlift under threat of extended prison sentences. This evidence suggests that Cuban government denials of deporting hardened criminals was a canard and figured into a state strategy for labeling the group as pathological. Eyewitness reports from those who went to Mariel and from the immigrants support the conclusion that a hard-core element was included in the migration. The evidence, however, suggests that the extent to which hard-core criminals infiltrated the migration was magnified by, on the one hand, the Cuban government's policy of ambiguity on the topic and, on the other hand, the U.S. media and bureaucratic responses to the Marielitos.

Official INS figures identified 1,306 "aliens" as having questionable backgrounds.[12] Scholars who have researched the criminal backgrounds of Mariel refugees have found that even among those identified as "hardened criminals" a significant number were in prison in Cuba for committing minor thefts and committing desperate acts of rebellion. The U.S. government's official figures presented to the U.N. were consistent with INS estimates. These estimates relied on the confessions and accusations of the émigrés since Cuban authorities refused to share legal and medical documents.

Similarly, the number of prisoners charged with petty crimes who "chose" to join the migration is uncertain. Up to 85% of the Marielitos did not have any prison records in Cuba, and the majority with prison records were incarcerated for minor crimes, which would not be considered crimes in the U.S., such as selling goods in the "black market."[13] Despite these figures, the pathological stereotype was successfully exported to the U.S. where it became magnified by the reception in America.

27

Closing Mariel

The Mariel migration ended suddenly on September 16, although the number of émigrés had declined significantly after the first week in June. The decreasing influx was due to a number of factors. For one, the costs to the ship owners involved in the Flotilla increased with the Carter Administration's policy of impounding vessels and fining ship owners. These risks also raised the costs to Cuban-Americans chartering vessels. Table 2 provides an overview of the exodus.

Table 2

Cuban Arrivals During the Mariel Exodus by Month, 1980

| | **Arrivals** | |
Month	Number	Percentage
April	7655	6.1
May	86,488	69.3
June	20,800	16.7
July	2629	2.1
August	3939	3.2
September	3258	2.6
Totals	124769	100

Source: Council for Inter-American Security, The 1980 Mariel exodus: An assesment and prospects, (Washington, D.C: Council for Inter-American Security, 1981),5.

Cuba's policies also discouraged Cuban-Americans who feared that they would not be allowed to find their relatives and might have to return with strangers and criminals. This fear contributed to the slowdown of the Flotilla, as did the policy of fining those chartering the ships. Cuba's press coverage of the negative experience of the Marielitos in the U.S., along with the high costs of departing Cuba, no doubt also influenced willingness to join the exodus.

The end of the migration responded most directly to the changing functions of the migration for the Cuban state. The port's closure coincided with well-timed and publicized actions aimed at showing Cuba's willingness to collaborate with the U.S. in dealing with illegal migration. On September 16, the Cuban government responded to a ninth hijacking since August 10 with the announcement that the pirating of planes to return to Cuba would lead "to drastic measures" including extradition. The following day, two young Cubans commandeered a Delta Airlines flight, diverting it to Havana. In an unprecedented act, the Cuban government extradited the hijackers to the U.S. GRANMA reported that this "drastic measure" demonstrated the seriousness of Cuba's commitment to cooperating on common problems between the two nations. The warm U.S. response to the Cuban's action reflected a changed diplomatic environment.

By September of 1980, Mariel stereotypes as pathological were well established. The Cuban state resorted to extraordinary measures to construct the "pathology" of the émigrés. The policy served the need of deflecting anxieties and fears in Cuba about the stability of the revolution and its future. In the history of the revolution, no migration was linked to the internal contradictions of socialism and primarily affected its "progeny." The extraordinary measures taken against the migrants reflected the need to reassure loyal supporters of the revolution and to excoriate its own rebellious offspring.

Furthermore, the portrayal of pathology also served the state's goal of turning the tables on its international vulnerability. Thus, the functions of deviance stereotype reflected the use of the migrants as a foreign policy tool to pressure the U.S. on a host of issues. The Cubans repeatedly used the negative stereotypes to highlight Cuba's anger over a U.S. immigration policy "rewarding those who commit crimes against the Cuban system." The Marielitos stigma thus served important state interests.

Political Context of the Marielitos Arrival in the U.S.

The Marielitos stigma transferred to the U.S. where it was

amplified. Mass public opinion, and the role of the U.S. media, played a critical role in this process. Mariel coincided with social and economic trends in the U.S. that were inimical to immigrants. This section reviews the role of public opinion, the role of the media and of organized interest groups in the process of transferring and amplifying the stigma.

In the U.S., the Marielitos immediate arrival coincided with an economic recession, which left millions of people unemployed and many others fearing a similar fate. More than seven million Americans were unemployed at the time of the Marielitos' arrival, a figure that was expected to rise to 10 million. The economic recession fed a furor over legal and illegal immigration, especially from Mexico, greater than any time since the Great Depression. The recession provided a context that was the "worst in the history of the exile" for Cuban arrivals.

Election year politics exacerbated the recession's political impact. Labor and minorities most affected by the recession, part of the Democratic party's political base, demanded tighter immigration controls especially toward illegal immigrants. The Carter administration responded to these demands by a general tightening of immigration regulations including doubling of the border patrol resources and cracking down on illegal immigrant smuggling rings. The large-scale influx of unscreened Cubans via the boatlift countered social conditions favoring stricter controls of immigrant flows. The refugees' untimely arrival contributed to the growing furor over perceived threats to jobs, increased welfare rolls, and economic security, posed by immigrants.

Fear of the émigrés fueled anti-immigrant feelings leading to what President Carter called an "unbelievable adverse reaction" to the émegrés. A survey conducted by the *Miami Herald* from May 1-4 showed that 70% of Americans interviewed perceived the influx of Cuban and Haitian immigrants as creating greater problems for the region. More than 80% of the African-Americans interviewed agreed with this assessment. African-Americans interviewed were also most likely to express fears of increased unemployment because of the arrivals from Mariel. The *Herald* survey found that, in contrast, more than 66% of the Hispanics interviewed believed that the émigrés would prove a boom to the area, suggesting that new arrivals set "state of interethnic and intercultural conflicts in the country."

The media amplified fears originating in Cuba about the alleged pathology of the migrants, especially their criminality, homosexual tendencies and delinquency. The media's representation overwhelmingly emphasized the alleged deviance. Typical were the *Nuevo Herald's* editorials between May 1 and August 30, 1980, dealing with Mariel. Content analysis of the editorials shows that one-third of all references to the Marielitos associated them with convicts and criminals and another twenty percent of the references associated them with mental illness. Less frequently used references to them as delinquents, ruffians and Castro agents made up another ten percent of the references.

Emphasis on the criminal threat posed by the Marielitos dominated the news coverage. Michael Daly of the *New York* magazine October 1980 Article, "Lost Bandidos Take the Town," for example, claims that "Castro drained his prisons into the 'Freedom Flotilla.'" Daly cites unnamed detectives in New York stating that there are "at least 2,000 gunmen who prowl the streets of New York operating in squads of four and five" committing rapes, murders and armed robberies. His sources stated there were 483 arrests of Marielitos in New York since the boatlift, representing "less than one tenth of the crimes actually committed."

The extent of danger to society posed by the Marielitos assumed significant dimensions in news accounts. For example, the *Miami Herald* argued that as many as 23,000 brought "experiences from Castro's jails" implying that, unlike previous "political prisoners" considered assets to the U.S., these posed a threat. The *Herald* reported that "the homicide rate in Miami jumped 66% the year of the Flotilla. The following year, the Marielitos accounted for 27% of Miami's 226 murder victims. One-third of those arrested and charged with murder in 1981 arrived via Mariel."[14]

The *U.S. News and World Report's* "Castro's Crime Bomb Inside the U.S." estimated that as many as 40,000 of the Marielitos were veterans of Castro's "brutal jails and mental hospitals." The Report went on to assert, based on the testimony of a "turncoat saboteur" that over 3,000 were Castro agents sent to the U.S. to run a "vast network for addicting Americans to drugs." Stressing the threat to public safety, the Report cites police sources in New York and Miami asserting that since 1980 there have been 7,000 and 3,232 arrests of Marielitos, respectively, in the two cities charged with "felonies, misdemeanors and criminal traffic violations."[15]

The news shared some common elements. Typically, the extent of the threat was left ambiguous for the reader. For example, the language used in reports frequently exaggerated the extent of the criminality by associating it with experience in Cuban jails affecting up to 40,000 or more of the migrants. Reports used such language as, for example, "veterans of Castro's brutal jails" to conjure images of the Marielitos as dangerous as a result of their past.

Case studies of Marielitos emphasized male criminals targeting female victims and involving acts of rape. Daly attributes much of the organized violence to the Marielitos' alleged links to Afro-Cuban cults such as beliefs in Changó and Oyá, which he claims leads the Marielitos to believe they are invincible criminals. The viciousness of the crimes reported, the code words associating the Marielitos with racial stereotypes of black crime, the emphasis on female victims, the connections to drugs and gangs reinforced negative stereotypes.

News reports of the Marielitos' criminal orientations, originating in Cuba, were often attributed to unnamed official sources in press reports. For example, on May 18, 1980, the *Arkansas Gazette* reported unnamed sources at Fort Chaffee stating that 25% of those screened to date had "questionable characters." Another report on June 1, 1980, claimed that of 10,376 émigrés screened, the INS has given a classification of "C" to 1,581, meaning that these individuals have a criminal record. On August 31, the Gazette once again cites INS agents as saying they "bent the INS rules on excluding criminals because there were so many. People who admitted to crimes were let go because there were too many to follow-up on... The majority of (the émigrés) were the dregs of Cuban society."

Local politicians blamed rising levels of crime on the Mariel émigrés. On September 22, 1980, Miami mayor, Maurice Ferré, for example, cited Dade County police statistics as showing a major increase in crime as a result of the Mariel immigrants "forcing the county to request aid of federal sources to confront the dramatic increase in crime." According to the mayor, the arrival of the Marielitos had caused increases of 774% in larcenies, 190% in armed robberies and 109% in violent crimes against persons in Little Havana."

A July 8 dispatch of the Associated Press reported on "U.S. organizations in defense of the rights of homosexuals who are trying to assist the thousands of their co-religionaires among the Cuban 'refugees' who came on the 'Freedom Flotilla." Another dispatch dated July 10 reported that the actual number of gay refugees is a matter of controversy among the social service agencies who are charged with their resettlement. It cited State Department officials as stating that the actual number is close to 20,000 of the 40,000 awaiting resettlement.[16]

The News Media and the Politics of Stigma

The phenomenon of stigmatization was linked to several political factors including "a naïve realism" among reporters covering the mass migration, favoring the representation of the émigrés in deviant terms.[17] Media "realism," reinforced by both U.S. and Cuban governmental sources, supported a cynical view of the émigrés to serve mutually advantageous political functions.

This perspective is supported by first-hand accounts of news reporting on the Mariel experience. James Conway, reporting for the *Atlantic Monthly*, visited Fort Chaffee in September of 1980. Conway reports on an incident involving a fist-fight among two camp interns recently consolidated at the Fort and the response which involved "the press, a ranking Public Affairs Office spokesman, a couple of bilingual soldiers, a paddy wagon, and six Police Park cars." Conway quotes a local Ft. Smith news reporter stating that "We haven't had any action in a long time. Now they're getting more people in. It's so much fun to cover this."

The Mariel stigma affirmed the dominant assumptions about the émigrés in U.S. society and ensured a receptive audience for the stories of the foreign "deviants" and "criminals." Other key factors that influenced the construction of the Marielitos' pathology included the election-year political pressures and frustrations in the Carter administration over the unwanted migration. Significant among these were the public backlash against liberal immigration policies and Cuba's continuing control of the ongoing boatlift, factors respectively from within and without the political system affecting attitudes at all levels of government.[18]

For the Carter administration, political pressures from Democratic party constituencies, such as labor and minority groups, and hostile public reaction to the émigrés, created political pressures to assume a get tough attitude on their legal status, conditions for resettlement, and deportation and incarceration policies towards Marielitos.

The Role of Interest Groups

Key Administration allies also called for a harsh response to the new arrivals. Meeting with President Carter in early May, Florida's congressional delegation criticized the Administration's posture of "open arms" toward the immigrants. An angry Dan Mica told President Carter that if he had met with delegation sooner, he would not "have made that comment in the way that you made it."[19] Even strong sympathizers of liberal admission of Cubans such as Senator Richard Stone, facing Senate reelection, suggested "the refugees be returned by force to Cuba where they would form a sort of fifth column fomenting rebellion against Castro or be intercepted off the Florida straits and sent to Costa Rica aboard Navy ships."[20]

The Administration also came under intense political attacks from political constituencies usually supportive of the President including labor, African-Americans and Latino groups. The initial influx of Marielitos led African-American advocacy groups to charge discriminatory treatment of the Haitians relative to Cubans. A number of groups had voiced the Haitian cause in the courts, the Congress and the press, among them the Haitian Refugee Center, the AFL/CIO, the Congressional Black Caucus, and the Mexican American Legal Defense and Educational Fund (MALDEF). The latter advocated the expansion of the refugee rubric to Mexicans arguing that economic hardship could be politically induced. One thrust of their efforts was to have the President grant asylum to Haitians whose parole was expiring on May 15.

Criticisms of the policies favoring émigrés from Cuba were voiced by Shirley Chisholm in the Congressional Black Caucus on June 17. Representative Chisholm argued that "one cannot separate the economic factors from the political ones... they are all interconnected." This argument challenged the Administration to generate a policy, which would ensure an equally favorable outcome for Haitians. Implicit and explicit charges of racism led David Crossland, the INS Commissioner, to testify before the immigration subcommittee that "race is not a factor."

Political hostility also came from some Latino Groups. *El Centro de la Raza* in a July 1980 report, asked rhetorically if "politically and morally we must ask ourselves if these antisocials who have arrived here out of their own greed and lack of patriotism should have equal or more equal access to the limited social services that our people have fought and sacrificed for." The Marielitos found few friends among Hispanics in the U.S. or few countervailing pressures to counteract their stigma.

The negative reaction against the Marielitos was also prevalent among significant sectors of the Cuban community in South Florida. A majority of the Cuban-Americans are members of the Republican Party, which was "using Mariel, and the presumed presence of deviants in it as a theme against Mr. Carter during the Presidential election." A majority of Cuban-Americans benefited from the close ties to the Republican Party, and stood to gain from the Party's promise of a more aggressive anti-Cuban foreign policy. These groups tacitly supported stigmatizing the Mariel immigrants to attack the Carter Administration's immigration and Cuba policies.

The intense criticisms of Marielitos from the media and organized interest groups, and a generally hostile public opinion created an environment ripe for transferring the Marielitos Cuban stigma and its amplification in U.S. society. The Carter Administration's policies fragmented in the face of intense public opinion and interest group pressures against the refugees, in part due to the conflict-avoidance of key policymakers as the negative reactions towards émegrés increased.[21] This situation led to a policy response that while striving for humane, lawful and fair treatment of immigrants, became mired in political and bureaucratic considerations that fed the stigmatization of the Cubans and which contributed to its amplification.

The Role of Political Elites

The Mariel exodus occurred in a political context that had been undergoing significant changes with regards to immigration attitudes and laws. The Carter Administration and the political leadership favored a change towards a refugee immigration policy more in line with the United Nations Convention on Refugees, based on equal treatment of individual asylum claims, and less influenced by Cold War considerations.

The legal context for Mariel was established when President Jimmy Carter signed The Refugee Act of 1980 a few weeks before the onset of the Mariel migration. The Act instituted what Senator Dante Fascell termed "the first comprehensive United States refugee resettlement and assistance policy" terminating the need for "ad hoc refugee programs such as the Cuban Refugee Program and the Indochinese Refugee Programs."

The Refugee Act set the context for new arrivals from Cuba. Prior to its enactment, refugee admissions policy, as illustrated by the Cuban example, responded primarily to Cold War considerations.[22] The Refugee Relief Act of 1953 reflected the Cold War mentality, expediting the admissions of refugees fleeing from communist-dominated countries in Europe and the U.S.S.R. This ideological bent was included in Amendments to the Immigration and Nationality Act of 1952 which expanded the definition of "refugee escapee" to include people in flight from communist or communist-dominated countries.

The Refugee Act of 1980 reflected the President's human rights concerns, and interest in a "comprehensive" refugee policy marking a shift in the attitudes of the governing elite towards refugees. The Act eliminated narrow geographical and ideological restrictions on refugee admissions, and authorized the entry for persons forced to depart their country because of persecution or well-founded fear of persecution because of race, religion, nationality, and membership in a particular social group or political opinion.[23]

The Act brought U.S. Refugee policy into compliance with U.N. human rights statutes, affirming Carter's commitment to multilateralism. It permitted President Carter to cast the Administration's refugee policy as "ideologically neutral" and as treating Cubans "as equal to those leaving other nations, whether Communist or noncommunist." The President would refer to the Act's ideological neutrality frequently during the Mariel migration insisting that "it is important to me that the Cuban and Haitian refugees be treated equally." President Carter's response in April and early May to the Mariel influx suggested he would use the authority of the Refugee Act to provide a legal entry for the Marielitos. On April 13, the President used his authority under Section 208 of the Refugee Act of 1980 to admit 3,500 Cubans who sought asylum at the Peruvian Embassy, about one-third of the Cubans at the Embassy. Three weeks after the opening of the port of Mariel, President Carter speaking at a press conference, indicated that "we'll continue to provide an open heart and open arms to refugees seeking freedom from Communist domination and from economic deprivations, brought about primarily by Fidel Castro and his government." Speaking for the Administration, Vice President Mondale commented that "there is no better proof of the failure of Castro's revolution than the dramatic exodus which is currently taking place." Such statements suggested the continuation of U.S. admission's leniency toward émigrés from Cuba.

The large inflow of refugees during the first three weeks of May, in a process largely controlled by the Cuban government and the illegal flotilla, forced the Administration to change its policy. Under the Act, granting an individual asylum involved initial review by the INS district directors, consultation with the State Department for advisory opinions, and in cases deemed doubtful by the State Department, an additional review by United Nations Commission on Refugees (UNCHR). In cases where the advisory opinion returned to the INS was negative, the applicant could raise the claim before an immigration judge and to a Board of Immigration Appeals. The continued use of the Refugee Act's asylum provisions and under Section 208 as the gateway for Mariel entrants required training hundreds of INS and State Department personnel in handling asylum reviews.

Apart from these administrative problems, the continued use of the asylum option had other drawbacks. For one, the option promised significant delays in resolving legal status and would leave individuals and localities without reimbursement for resettlement expenses. For another, the policy would likely discriminate against the Haitians less likely to meet the INS standards for persecution under the Act's terms undermining the President's commitment to "ideological neutrality." These problems caused the Administration to rethink its approach and led to demands that President Carter use less stringent criteria for granting refugee status, relying on different provisions in the Refugee Act to deal with the crisis. Senator Edward Kennedy, Chair of the Senate Judiciary Committee and a rival to President Carter for the Democratic Party nomination, argued for using the Refugee Act's emergency provisions under Section 207 to extend blanket refugee status on humanitarian grounds. This approach was also advocated by Representative Peter Rodino, Chair of the House of Representative's Immigration Committee.

Section 207 permitted the President in consultation with the House and Senate Judiciary Committees to establish separate administrative criteria for screening and granting admission. Individuals who did not qualify as refugees would be illegal entrants and could be excluded or resettled in other countries. Responsibility for implementing the guidelines rested on the Attorney General Benjamin Civeletti, and through him on INS officers and voluntary agency personnel in the field. This approach simplified the admissions review process enlisting the support of private voluntary organizations, and state and local agencies. It identified the range of services available to the émigrés, the levels of federal reimbursement to state, local and private agencies (for example, hospitals) and set forth the administrative oversight of the resettlement process. The Marielitos status as refugees would resemble that of the previous waves of Cuban émigrés admitted to the U.S.

Use of Section 207 required President Carter to make a

finding of a "humanitarian emergency." The Act provided the President discretionary authority to admit an additional 50,000 refugees over the agreed upon limit (217,000 in 1981). Under emergency provisions, the President, in consultation with Congress, could increase the cap in any fiscal year by a number appropriate to deal with unforeseen "emergency" refugee situations.

Interest group and public opposition to this course precipitated an intense intra-elite debate within the Carter Administration, eventually leading to a new ad hoc entrant designation for the Cubans. There was considerable opposition in the House of Representatives to the use of the humanitarian emergency provisions. Representative Elizabeth Holtzman of New York, head of the House Committee on Immigration, argued for "extreme caution" in the review of the émigrés claiming "that as many as 700 ex-convicts had been rounded up by the Cuban Government and given the choice of going to the United States or back to jail."

Efforts to coordinate policy were hampered by divisions among the Administration elites, especially between the State Department and Democratic constituencies , favoring a strict adherence to asylum laws for the Cubans, and officials in Health and Human Services and some Democratic leaders, such as Senator Edward Kennedy, who favored using the Refugee Act to grant asylum to the group. Within the Administration, Secretary of State Cyrus Vance, opposed extending refugee status to the refugees arguing that this option opened the possibility for large numbers from other countries to seek similar treatment. Concerns over the impact of extending asylum status to the Cubans on race relations in the U.S. further contributed to the abandonment of this provision in the Act.

The conflict over the new arrivals delayed the Carter Administration's decision as to their legal status until June 20, over two months after the opening of Mariel Harbor. The decision to declare the Cubans as "excludable aliens" under a new administrative designation of "entrant" marked a dramatic departure from the Refugee Act and created a different status for the arrivals and created the context for bureaucratic fragmentation of authority and responsibility for the immigrants.

Initially, the Administration bought time by tasking the Federal Emergency Management Agency with the first line response to the émigrés' arrival and centralizing coordination of the crisis in the President's Special Assistant, Jack Watson. As the exodus escalated, an Ad Hoc Cuban-Haitian Task Force was created under the State Department's Coordinator of Refugee Affairs, Victor Palmieri. The Task Force was charged with preparing a plan for an inter-agency response to the crisis, which would address the political dimensions of the problem.

The decision to relegate management of the Mariel migrants to a relatively weak and understaffed agency while locating overall decision authority in the White House set the stage for policy incoherence. As the political controversies surrounding the Marielitos in the U.S. intensified, those responsible for the overall policy at the strategic level, Domestic Policy Advisor Eugene Eizenstadt and National Security Advisor Zbigniew Brzezinski distanced themselves from the issue, which became a political land mine.[24] In this context, the Carter Administration's response was increasingly fragmented, allowing political and bureaucratic interests at the level of the military and local police agencies, the INS, and local agencies to dominate policy making. The amplification of the stigma of the Marielitos and their experiences at detention camps such as Ft. Chaffee was closely related to this policy incoherence. In this setting, those interest groups and bureaucracies most antithetical to the immigrants and most likely to amplify negative stereotypes of the Marielitos dominated the agenda.

The evidence suggests that, not unlike what happened in Cuba, bureaucracies in the U.S. benefited from the stigmatization of Marielitos. Bureaucratic interests concerned with avoiding the risk of antagonizing interests groups and negative public opinion, maximized their own political support by exaggerating the refugee negative stereotypes. Scholarship on this topic suggests that the INS and other agencies pursued measures calculated to reinforce public fears of the Marielitos and to use this as a means to gain public support for increased law enforcement budgets and for tough treatment of immigrants.[25]

While serving different purposes in Cuba and the U.S., the stigmatization of the émegrés benefited powerful interests in both societies.

The Development of the Mariel Stigma at Ft. Chaffee

This section on Ft. Chaffee presents an extended discussion of the Mariel's experience in this resettlement camp. The focus on Chaffee is based on the significance of the camp in defining the stigma of pathology in the national consciousness. A large number of the Marielitos, almost 55%, were sent to detention camps in Florida, Pennsylvania, Wisconsin and Arkansas to be screened and processed. Ft. Chaffee was the largest of the camps and the final processing site for the Cubans considered hard to sponsor. Nearly 25,000 Marielitos were interned at Fort Chaffee during the period from May 9, 1980, to January 31, 1982. Cubans at Fort Chaffee were variously portrayed as "trouble-makers," "promiscuous homosexuals," "gang members," "agents" and "antisocial," contributing significantly to the pathological stereotype.

The Chaffee experience demonstrates the role of local political elites in the development of the national stereotype. It also provides insight into the many obstacles that the refugees were to face post-resettlement. The many traumatic experiences in the camps, the labels and records that many were to carry with them after resettlement, the willingness to use extraordinary social control measures were based on the fears and political pressures engendered by their stigma. Marielitos at Chaffee caused local officials to deal with critical issues related to the treatment of the Cubans, the legal and human rights implications of detention, and internal (to the camp) and external security issues raised by the camp population. Decisions at Ft. Chaffee set a tone for the treatment of Marielitos and a lens with which to view the future prospects of many of them in the U.S.

Ft. Chaffee's selection as a resettlement site was not a random act. The Fort had served as an immigrant-processing center during the 1940's when Japanese citizens were held there. In the mid 1970's, Indochinese refugees were brought to the camp to be screened and relocated throughout the U.S. The camp's facilities and its personnel had accommodated large-scale refugee resettlement efforts in the past and were suited to deal with a large influx of immigrants.

The case of the Cuban migrants, however, occurred in a political and bureaucratic context different from the resettlement experiences of the 1970's. The intense negative reaction to the Marielitos and the political pressures on camp personnel affected their goal orientations making security concerns primary. Internal conflicts between service and security goal-oriented agencies fostered a sense of bureaucratic competition over security measures, which, in turn, fed the media portrayals of the refugees.

The vast majority of the Marielitos spent anywhere from two weeks to less than three months at the camp and were not associated with the disturbances or criminal behaviors used to stigmatize the group. Between May 9 and June 3, 1980, 19,041 immigrants were processed through the camp with 562 of the immigrants permitted to depart the camp during that period. Following the camp disturbances in late May and early June, the rate of sponsorship mostly by family and friends decreased the camp population rapidly. By August of 1980, the camp population had decreased to 3,178. The October 1980 consolidation at Fort Chaffee of 6,000 hard-to-place Marielitos from other campsites increased the Ft. Chaffee population to 8,310. The number of detained Cubans declined between October 1980 and March of 1981 to 2,252. By June of 1981, there were 1,600 Marielitos at Ft. Chaffee with the vast majority being single black males with few if any job skills and little formal education. The majority was identified as having "prison records or psychiatric histories." This number fell further to 586 by August of 1981 after which time the camp was effectively transformed into a "holding center" with 415 Marielitos eventually transferred to federal prisons.

Ft. Chaffee became the third largest city in Arkansas. Life at the camp, at first, took on a celebratory character recreating many social and cultural activities brought from Cuba (as may be seen in the photographs). Many traditional Cuban sports such as baseball and boxing, games such as dominos, and cultural and religious practices were recreated in the camp, creating a mini-Cuban community in the Ozarks. The presence of families and children and the active camp "black market" in jeans, cigarettes and other commodities made for a diversified and dynamic community.

The behaviors linked to Mariel stereotype were more prevalent following the October 10 consolidation of Cubans at Fort Chaffee. Official data suggests that 78% of the assaults and stabbings attributed to the Ft. Chaffee Cubans as a whole occurred in the four months after the October consolidation when most of the Marielitos originally processed through the camp had been released. Both of the murders reported at Fort Chaffee during the entire Ft. Chaffee internment of Cubans also occurred during that four-month period. The increase in aggressive behaviors was, in turn, linked to tensions connected to the dwindling rates of resettlement after October.

As indicated, resettlement rates fell dramatically following the consolidation in October. As a confidential June 1981 memorandum states, "the outlook of each remaining entrant is exacerbated by frustrations with the monotony of camp routine, uncertainty over the future and knowledge gleaned from the media that policy regarding them is muddled. As the population diminished, the self-image of the entrant declines."

The Mariel stereotype drew heavily on the experience of those few Cubans with prolonged camp internment, especially the minority criminal element that preyed on others and the acts of frustrated individuals who did not understand the reasons for their prolonged internment at the camp. However, the stereotype was not created primarily by acts of criminality or of desperation but preceded them and stigmatized the entire Mariel population. The stigmatization of the Cubans at Fort Chaffee preceded their arrival at the Fort and was amplified by the propensity of local political leaders, the media and public opinion to portray all forms of Marielito protest as evidence of pathological behavior. The immigrants were largely powerless to influence the public construction of their experiences as pathological and the few who sought to speak on their behalf were largely silenced by the political climate of hostility to the immigrants.

Arrival at the Fort

The first Cubans arrived at the camp on May 9 amidst growing controversies over the decision to use Ft. Chaffee as a
screening and resettlement center. There were conflicting
reports on Ft. Chaffee's role in the refugee flow. Rumors in the
local press reported that President Carter might be admitting
more than 250,000 Cubans and another 250,000 Haitians
into the country and there were conflicting estimates as to how
many Cubans would be sent to Fort Chaffee. On May 8, in its
announcement that the Fort would be used to screen Cubans,
White House officials indicated that as many as 15,000
Cubans would be sent to the camp. On May 12, military officials at the camp were predicting as many as 20,000 would
arrive, and on the next day officials estimated that as many as
25,000 would be arriving. Adding to uncertainty over the
Fort's resettlement role, on May 9, White House officials
reported that all Cubans transferred to the Fort would be
screened for criminals in Miami, and that criminals would not
be sent to the fort. As the refugee flow increased, however, this
policy was reversed and the decision made to send Cubans to
Ft. Chaffee without prior screening. Mixed and sometimes
conflicting messages about the Cubans being sent to Ft.
Chaffee contributed to fear.

Initial reactions in Arkansas to the opening of Chaffee as a
resettlement center indicate the impact of the pathological
stereotype on local political elites and on public opinion.
Initial positive coverage of the migrants in the media was
reflected in Governor Bill Clinton's announcement at a May 8
press conference in Little Rock that "the Cuban refugees who
are now temporarily housed in Florida came to this country in
flight from a Communist dictatorship. I know that everyone in
this state sympathizes and identifies with them in their desire
for freedom." The Governor promised to do all that he could
to "fulfill whatever responsibilities the President imposes
upon Arkansas to facilitate the refugees' resettlement."

As news coverage accentuated the criminal and patholog-
cal, the Governor expressed a more cautious stance indicating
that the federal government should set up offshore screening

sites and proposing the relocation of refugees without family ties to third countries. Other Arkansas state officials criticized the White House's decision to use the Fort as a center for refugee screening. The Congressional representative for the Fort Smith region, John Paul Hammerschmidt, had tried to dissuade the White House from using Fort Chaffee for screening. The Congressman lamented that the refugee problem should not be a burden on "Fort Chaffee or Arkansas or just America." Representative Bill Alexander expressed concerns that federal authorities "provide proper consideration to the winnowing out of criminals, mental patients, Castro agents and provocateurs that might prey on innocent Americans."[26] Similarly, Fort Smith mayor, Jack Freeze, was quoted as saying that he did not think that the Cubans would be as well received as the Vietnamese refugees, "because of the unknown quality of these people."[27] He added that stories in the press had "led us to believe these people are undesirable types." Sounding a deep note of alarm, Senator Dale Bumpers suggested that the current U.S. immigration policy threatened, "to disrupt our whole democratic process." These comments contributed to the fearful climate among residents of the Ft. Smith area.

The first Cuban arrivals at Ft. Chaffee on May 9 were transplanted into an increasingly hostile environment. The earliest press accounts of the new immigrants at the Fort highlighted public health threats posed by the Cubans. The *Arkansas Gazette* cited unnamed sources saying that medical teams were finding high rates of disease among the Cubans.[28] Rumors of serious illnesses among the new arrivals continued to be reported throughout May despite evidence that medical screening of the refugees was being delayed by lack of medical personnel and equipment, and denials from FEMA representative, McAda, and spokespersons from the Public Health Service conducting the medical screening. The focus on public health threats continued throughout the summer despite State Department Bulletin announcements indicating that, "the general health of the Cuban population at the Fort is good."[29]

The news also focused on the criminality of the immigrants. Local reports in the *Gazette* that Cuban officials were emptying jails and asylums and forcing criminals and provocateurs to join the boatlift fueled fears around Ft. Smith and neighboring communities. Press reports in Arkansas cited the inclusion of criminals in the boatlift and the detention of criminal elements at South Florida's Federal Correctional Institute. Press reports that initial screening of Cubans showed that 25% had "questionable" backgrounds were given credibility by citing federal and local officials concerned about the Cubans. State Department official, Harry Johnson, was cited suggesting that it might be necessary to repatriate criminals to a "third communist country" if Cuba would not accept their return. Representative Bill Alexander, on May 13, cited evidence he had collected from boat captains participating in the refugee exodus indicating that criminals were being forced onto the refugee boats and urged that the Cubans be held in the camps until positive identifications had been made.[30] These comments conveyed a sense of urgent threat to public order and safety from the Marielitos at the Fort.

The local papers' coverage in May and June focused on alleged criminal behaviors inside Chaffee. Press reports of "increasing larcenies and other disturbances" in the camp, along with incidents of some refugees leaving the camp further raised local fears of the Cubans. On May 22, Captain Delion Causey of the State Police Headquarters at Fort Smith claimed that residents in the area were "pretty scared" and warned about Cubans being picked up in downtown Fort Smith.[31]

Negative stereotyping fed on contradictory comments from local officials. For example, the *Gazette* cited an INS official, Ronald Brooks, stating that "there are no more criminals in this bunch than if you'd go out on the street and pick up 500 people at random."[32] Such statements, juxtaposed with the comments of other officials and local politicians left the impression that no one knew who the Cubans were or of government misinformation.

New accounts of local hostile reactions ranged from those of "mainstream" politicians and local leaders to extremist elements of the KKK. In mid-May, a Klan contingent, led by David Duke, began to stage protest demonstrations outside the camp and incidents of KKK activities at the airport through which Cubans passed in route to the camp were reported.[33] At the

46

same time, local police were quoted about growing community fears and Steve Lease, the Fort Smith City Administrator,
warned that residents were "armed and waiting." The spectacle thus constructed the extreme reactions to the Marielitos as
having mainstream support validating the perception of
threat. Reports that some Cubans were leaving the Fort without permission set the stage for political demands to maximize security goals aimed at containment of the Marielitos.

The Stigma's Impact on Camp Security

Stigmatization created significant political pressures to
change screening and resettlement procedures and to emphasize the containment of "threat" within the camp. The stigma
of the Marielito led to significant changes in the political functions of the resettlement experience. Fear of new immigrants
led to considerable changes in their treatment during the
screening and resettlement phase. Changes reflected the contradictions in camp policies emanating from the need to relocate the migrants with sponsors and the pressures to contain
the perceived Marielito threat.

The stigma was fed, in part, by the actions of the immigrants themselves who failed to understand or acquiesce in
the different treatment they were receiving. Inside the camp,
there was increasing malaise with delays in processing,
including those with family sponsors. The Cubans' frustration
over the internment increased throughout the period. On May
27, between 300 and 400 fled the camp and headed down the
main highway toward Ft. Smith. Most were rounded up by the
state police the next day. On May 31, another 1,000 Cubans
rushed the main gate of the camp seeking to leave Chaffee
where they were met by federal officers armed with M16's and
tear gas. An additional 300 Cubans threatened to go on a
hunger strike. The next day, 40 Cubans participated in a sit-
down protest demanding to see their relatives at an American
Red Cross center. Family members outside the Fort also
joined in the protest activity. David Lewis, Director of United
States Catholic Charities (UCSC) at the Fort, attributed the
tensions to delays in releasing refugees, confusion between the
Immigration and Naturalization Service (INS) and FEMA in

processing refugees, and the Cubans growing tired of waiting. By June 3, camp officials had granted 2,400 refugees clearance to leave the installation, but only 562 had been permitted to leave.

June 1 Uprising

The June 1 uprising in the camp caught camp and local officials by surprise and marked a turning point in the stigmatization of the Marielitos. There were early signs that conditions were nearing a crisis. The day before, Víctor Valdés of Chicago, a former Cuban political prisoner who was serving at the request of camp officials as an intermediary between the refugees and the resettlement officials, had told an angry group of Cubans that they should "broaden" their protests and accused camp officials of lying about the timetable for releasing screened immigrants. As tensions increased the next day, police had fired shots and some Cubans had thrown stones at security personnel. By midday, 2,000 Cubans were rioting and said to be roaming the camp armed with clubs, according to FEMA Coordinator McAda. Angry protestors burned four buildings, two of these mess halls, and more than 200 busted out of the camp and headed toward the nearby city of Barling.[34]

The protestors met with armed resistance outside the city limits. A group of 100 encountered a police roadblock where a skirmish occurred with the police. Police troopers rushed the crowd wielding nightsticks, turning most back toward the Fort's main gate. Another group circumvented the police roadblock but was met by troops with raised guns. Shots were fired into the air causing the refugees to stampede back toward the camp. Early reports indicated that 15 troopers and 4 refugees had been injured in the fighting. Later reports indicated five Cubans had been shot during the uprising.

The protestors provoked an angry reaction by Barling residents. A contingent of 300 to 400 armed citizens gathered near the city limits and were threatening to "rush the compound and kill those ****." The local commander of the State Police asked the crowd to give the police a chance to control the situation and "if we can't, we will welcome your help."

State officials also called for emergency detention and arrest powers to deal with the Cubans leaving the Fort.[35] Local political officials' heightened security concerns led them to challenge legal rulings by both the Federal and State Attorney General that Cubans leaving the Fort were not committing a crime and could not be arrested. Steve Lease, the City Administrator, said local officials would continue to pick up Cubans.

The June 1 uprising led Governor Clinton, who toured the camp by helicopter, to declare emergency measures, including the suspension of leaves for all state troopers and to call for increased security procedures within the camp. The Governor and local political officials sought to limit the political damage caused by increasingly hostile and fearful public opinion by pressuring federal camp administrators to tighten security procedures. The political function of the camp was to ensure that local voters understood that the immigrant danger was being contained using all necessary force.[36] The photographs on pages 98-99 show police forces amassing on the camp grounds and also show the transformation of the camp from an open facility to one with barbed wire perimeter.

In response, a stockade was established and 97 of the refugees identified as leaders of the uprising were detained. The riots prompted President Carter to announce that no more refugees would be sent to the camp. Public demands for security voiced by Governor Clinton led to the installation of new razor wire fences around the camp's perimeter. As fears of the Cubans mounted in the area, Governor Bill Clinton dispatched increasing numbers of state troopers to guard the camp. Following the May 27 breakout of Marielitos from the camp, the Governor called the National Guard on alert and demanded the deportation of anyone rioting. An angry Clinton told federal officials they had 72 hours to tighten security and ordered the National Guard to aid the police. He also demanded that more authority be given to the military police to arrest escaping refugees and divulged that an additional 75 General Service Administration security personnel would join the state police, state troopers and federal police in addition to the National Guard troops, including 175 Puerto Rican National Guard members flown to the camp in mid-May. Clinton advisor, Tommy Robinson, a former Public Safety Director for the state, advised the Governor that an additional 20 state troopers were needed immediately at the camp. Steve Lease, the Fort Smith City Administrator, warned that state and local officials "would control what federal officials obviously cannot."

The June uprising and the social and political tensions generated by the Cubans' unrest underscored to the Carter Administration the political liabilities in the existing bureaucratic response to the crisis, especially the lack of coordination of policies and procedures. Bureaucratic conflicts between FEMA, the INS and the FBI over the management of the camp and of relations with local communities was contributing to the news in ways that were increasing the political costs of the migration. Conflicting images of the Cubans heightened insecurity among those who wanted tighter controls over the camp population. This situation and its attendant political costs led to major changes in camp personnel, policies and procedures after June 1 which effectively transformed the camp into a detention center and gave local authorities unprecedented discretion in managing the Mariel immigrants.

Changes in camp personnel and procedures for resettlement exemplified the changing character of the Fort. Moved to action by the unrest of the refugees, INS official, Ed Cavin, head of operations at the Fort, initiated changes to help speed the resettlement process allowing Cubans with family sponsors to be resettled in communities before completing their FBI screening. This process increased the speed of resettlement allowing 538 Cubans to be resettled in the first five days after the uprising.

Beginning on June 10, top Fort officials were replaced, security tightened and procedures requiring full clearance from the FBI and Washington, D.C. reinstituted.[37] A group of 55 "hardcore troublemakers" identified as leaders of the uprising were transferred to El Paso, Texas holding area. Governor Clinton demanded the transfer of all the Cubans stockaded in the camp.

Following the uprising, FEMA Coordinator Bill Tidball and FEMA Public Relations Officer McAda were replaced by new

FEMA officials because they had reportedly lost credibility with local residents. McAda's comments before the uprising had minimized the problems of Cubans leaving the Fort, and favored existing security arrangements more generally. FEMA had been assigned principal responsibility for coordinating the response to the Mariel crisis, including the screening and resettlement of the Cubans by the Carter Administration. INS official Ron Brooks came under criticism for relaxing screening procedures and was put under a new INS supervisor. Bill Traugh, the new FEMA Director at the Fort, declared, "no one will be released without a full clearance." The number of released refugees dropped to fewer than 55 a day after reaching record numbers for the camp following the uprising. Reversing an earlier decision not to transfer those seen as responsible for the uprising from the camp, the INS sent 37 additional Cubans to the Atlanta Federal Penitentiary.

By mid July, a new inter-agency task force was established to play a coordinating role in the reception, resettlement, camps operation and attendant work with the national voluntary agencies (VOLAGS). The Cuban-Haitian Task Force, under the Office of Refugee Affairs in the Department of State (later transferred to the Department of Health and Human Services), would through its Fort Chaffee office, assume responsibility for dealing with the Marielitos at Fort Chaffee.

Local Elite Responses to Mariel Cubans

A turning point came in late July after the White House's decision to consolidate refugees housed at Ft. McCoy, Fort Eglin and Fort Indiantown Gap at the Chaffee installation. The approximately 10,000 Cubans consolidated at Chaffee were variously portrayed as hard-core gang members, prostitutes, criminals and deviants posing an imminent threat of violence. This stereotype was largely accepted as truth and led to intensified pressures to further militarize the camp to ensure the security of the surrounding populations. The stigma and attendant security measures fostered a negative climate for resettlement.

The July 26 announcement by Governor Clinton that the White House had asked him to "volunteer" the use of the Fort

51

as a consolidation center for hard-to-place refugees was accompanied by speculation that the Carter administration was minimizing the electoral costs of the Cuban boatlift for the upcoming elections.[38] Consolidation of the Cubans in one site was said to minimize the electoral costs to the President relative to a more dispersed camp situation. Governor Clinton reacted negatively to the request indicating that his initial response would be "no", but that he would consult with local authorities "because of the economic benefits the refugee center has brought to the area." Sebastian County Sheriff Bill Cauthron reflected much of the local attitude when he said that he "did not want four thousand homosexuals released into Fort Smith" and worried that the camp might become a vocational center releasing "rehabilitated" refugees into the community.[39]

Despite this initial hostile reaction, the Carter Administration decided to use Fort Chaffee as a consolidation site (on August 7) amidst angry local reactions. The Administration's decision was apparently made without significant consultation with local officials. Governor Clinton claimed that he found out about the decision after the fact when he called Presidential Assistant Eidenberg to discuss planned reductions of military forces at the camp. He reported telling Eidenberg that the decision was a "bad mistake." Similarly, Congressman Pryor reported that he found out about the decision by "accident" when one of his aides contacted the White House on an unrelated matter.[40]

The reaction of local leaders to the White House's decision was hostile. Governor Clinton called the decision "outrageous" and Fort Smith mayor Jack Freeze, angrily called the decision a betrayal of a "Governor, two senators and a congressman." Country Judge Bob Boyer said that the people here overwhelmingly disapproved and "we told Washington that." Other local officials indicated they wanted nothing to do with the situation and that the Army should handle the refugees "if they can." An angry Congressman Pryor warned the Carter Administration that the decision "would be devastating for President Carter's election in Arkansas." Governor Clinton promised to meet with White House officials to try to reverse the decision, but gave little hope that he would succeed in this effort. Press reports following the consolidation decision once again emphasized the anger of local residents to the use of the Fort for "undesirables dumped by Castro."

White House officials sought to minimize tensions promising to consult with the Governor and local officials in planning of the security measures for the camp. On August 5, President Carter went further implicitly giving Governor Clinton veto authority over the security arrangements of the Fort.[41] The President reportedly told the Governor "if security arrangements were not satisfactory, they would be changed until they met his approval." A task force consisting of federal officials, including the military commander of the Fort, and local officials began planning security at the camp with the charge from the Governor to provide him with a list of "minimum" security conditions that must be met. This planning group would be responsible for the tightening of camp security and the eventual transformation of the installation into a de facto prison, cementing the negative stereotype of the Marielitos and turning the camp into a symbol of the group's stigma.

Local officials expressed dissatisfaction with the federal government's proposed management of the relocation center from the start. In a first meeting with Carter's Coordinator of Refugee Affairs, Eugene Eidenberg, Ft. Smith Mayor Freeze indicated concerns with federal policies, which shifted responsibility for refugee assistance to the local level once refugees were sponsored out of the camp. He expressed concern about Cubans drifting back to Ft. Smith without sponsors and becoming "local problems." Freeze indicated that local authorities had agreed to receive Cubans at the airport and bus stations but that "we did not want them to stay in Fort Smith or come back." The main concerns in the meetings, however, focused on camp security.

The White House's plan to relocate Cubans into Chaffee by mid-September, before the onset of the cold weather in Wisconsin and Pennsylvania, was thwarted by Arkansas officials who insisted on approving all security provisions surrounding the transfer. On August 25, state officials asked the State Department to delay the transfer while security arrangements were detailed. Governor Clinton announced that he expected at least a two-week delay until the planning group could present him with a security plan. Clinton began to lay out the initial security conditions that needed to be met before giving his consent, including immediate notification of state and local authorities of any disturbances and the establishment of a central communication center to transmit and receive radio frequencies monitored by state and local police officers. Eventually the governor would propose a list of 19 conditions to be met.

Deliberations over security conditions occurred in the context of news indicating that security might decline because of the Army's pullout from the camp. The Army's growing discontent with its role in a civilian operation led to statements indicating the desire to reduce its presence at the camp from 150 to 100, leaving the Federal Park Police with the primary responsibility for maintaining order. There were also reports from unnamed INS officials who lamented that the INS was bending its own rules on excluding criminals at the Fort because there were so many and claimed that "the majority were dregs of Cuban society." These reports further heightened fears and led to demands for more security guarantees from Arkansas officials. Congressman Hammerschmidt fired off an angry letter to the White House denouncing the reported military stand down as yet another broken promise to the State.

The alliance of local Democratic officials, especially Governor Clinton, the news and public opinion brought political pressure to bear on the President. On September 6, the White House announced that there would not be any troop reductions at Fort Chaffee and specifying the time for military deployment at the Fort, contradicting the Army's position on its role in the consolidation process. The construction of a thirteen-foot fence around the camp area housing the refugees also sought to tighten security conditions, as illustrated in photographs 12 and 13. Despite these developments, on September 11, Governor Clinton blocked the transfer of refugees to the Fort citing problems with the security plan and setting conditions for refugee consolidation, including the guarantee that troublemakers would be screened before the relocation to Chaffee and that these cases should not be sent to Arkansas.

Over the next few weeks, conflicts within the security-planning group caused further delays in the refugee consolidation with local authorities demanding tighter security as a precondition for consenting to a plan. On September 12, Eidenberg announced an agreement with Clinton that included: the reimbursement of state and local expenditures including the damage done to the Fort during the June uprising; the exclusion of new arrivals from Cuba; the authority for the Army to use force if necessary and its agreement to take on a more "interventionist" role in the management of the Cubans; and, the expansion of relief services in the camp to make them more sponsorable.[42] The Governor also demanded that refugee transfers from the Fort Smith airport to the camp occur in daylight form 9:00 a.m. to 3:00 p.m. to minimize the dangers of escapes and riots.

This agreement on the security conditions was overtaken by reports of conditions at other camps, especially a report by Kramer Schwars of the Public Health Service on conditions at McCoy. The report warned of gang wars at the Fort and about the probable need to use force to transfer reluctant McCoy refugees who are fearful of the situation at Chaffee. Protests at Fort Chaffee on September 16 including the burning of a barrack and the reported discovery of a load of knives and "junk that could be used as weapons" undermined support for the security plan. In this context, Governor Clinton demanded additional security measures at the camp.

The new demands included the development of a Special Security Advisory Group composed of local officials appointed by the Governor with responsibility to screen incoming Cubans, indicating the continued State distrust of federal officials' promises to screen troublemakers. The Governor also demanded that this group be given complete access to Fort Chaffee and to have final say on all security agreements, including troop reductions at the camp. The Governor also demanded a periodic count of the camp population to assure authorities about the continuing incidence of attempted flights from the Fort, and demanded the appointment of an overall coordinator of operations accountable for camp management. Other demands included: limiting the number of refugees transferred to 10,000; the return of all refugees losing sponsors to the camp; meeting the concerns of Mayor Freeze to exclude the Cubans from community; and the use of the military in guarding the Cubans transported from the airport to the camp.

On September 16, Christopher Holmes, Director of the Cuban-Haitian Task Force of the State Department responded to the Governor. Holmes agreed to most of the conditions, but indicated that access to the Fort was under the authority of the military and could not be delegated to the Advisory group. He further indicated that the administration would consult with the Governor on troop reductions and the use of force, but stated that final authority for these matters was in the Departments of Defense and Justice. Holmes' response led Captain Deloin Causey to criticize the security plan as ambiguous and to demand that the federal government clearly explain the military's role in policing the camp.[43] He further demanded clarification of the authority of state police officials to arrest refugees for leaving the camp, warning that "we can't have a bunch of illegal aliens roaming around the community. We're going to have to move on it and argue the legal niceties later."

The ongoing disputes over a security plan led Governor Clinton on September 19 to call for a more detailed plan. The Governor, echoing Captain Delion's protests, indicated that he would ask Attorney General Steve Clark to rule on the authority of state and local authorities to arrest refugees outside the camp, despite the absence of legal sanctions prohibiting the entrants from leaving the camp.[44] The high level of distrust and anger between federal, state and local officials placed the consolidation strategy of the White House in an administrative limbo.

Ironically, calls for increased security in the camp belied the real conditions of insecurity being experienced by the Marielitos, especially those individuals and families whose only problem was that they did not have relatives in the U.S., and were finding sponsorship difficult due stereotyping. As the camp's operation was transformed into a prison-like environment, difficulties with finding sponsors also increased.

Political Elite Fractures over the Marielitos

The September 24 meeting between Governor Clinton, members of his staff and advisors including Sebastian County Sheriff Bill Cauthron, Arkansas National Guard Colonel Bill Cook and State Police Captain Delion Causey, and Cuban Haitian Task Force Charles Cain, Paul Michele, Assistant Attorney General for the Justice Department and Army Brigadier General James Moore, produced an agreement on the security arrangements for the consolidation. A wary Governor Clinton called the agreement "acceptable but not perfect."

Deliberations focused on the frayed trust and perceived lack of communication between federal and state officials. The agreement designated Colonel Cook as the "liaison" between federal and state officials (including Governor Clinton), and determined the degree of access he would have to the camp. The agreement left open-ended the matter of the legal authority of state and local officials to arrest Cubans who might leave the Fort without permission, a matter that was under study by State Attorney General Steve Clark. Extraordinary security measures were the quid pro quo for the agreement, including requiring all refugees losing sponsors in the area to return to the camp. The agreement also included provisions that would exclude mental patients, juveniles and "potential troublemakers from the consolidation."

Apparently, these measures satisfied local authorities and Clinton reported that his acceptance of the deal "was based primarily on the confidence expressed by Police Captain Causey and Sheriff Cauthron." Authority over camp security policies was effectively transferred to the Security Advisory Group, and especially the law enforcement personnel appointed by the Governor. Their access to the Governor through his liaison with public safety agencies, Robert Lyford, gave this group a considerable amount of power over the consolidation process and policy.

The decision to consolidate the Cubans at the Fort led to prompt action on the part of Federal authorities to begin the consolidation of 3,000 Cubans remaining at Fort McCoy, an additional 3,000 at Indiantown Gap, Pennsylvania, and 800 at

Fort Eglin, Florida. Within 24 hours of Clinton's accession to the consolidation, 613 Cubans were transferred to Fort Chaffee. The consolidation was marked by political controversies from the start and would cause significant political embarrassment to the Governor. Major problems erupted when Attorney General Steve Clark announced on September 26 that, in his legal opinion, the arrest or detention of Cuban refugees leaving the camp was illegal stating further "all can leave if they wish."[45]

Clark's formal opinion filed as an official report and communicated by letter to the Governor held that President Carter did not have the authority to allow the entry of 114,000 Cubans into the U.S. and that the Mariel Cubans were illegally in the country. As illegal, never given status as "refugee, immigrants or aliens," the federal government could not force the refugees to stay at the Fort. Clark went on to add that state and local authorities did not have the power to arrest Cubans for merely leaving the camp. According to Clark, "Six thousand Cubans walking on Highway 22 aren't guilty of anything," and he further stated that "he was unaware of any law in this state which would prohibit or makes it a crime for an alien person to leave a federal compound without permission." He warned that a person illegally detained could sue in federal court and the arresting officer "could expect to be prosecuted."

Clark's opinion also questioned the use of the Fort as a detention center since it had not been officially designated by the Carter Administration for this purpose. The State Attorney General urged the Governor to ask the U.S. Attorney General Benjamin Civeletti to assign a legal status to the Cubans and to designate Fort Chaffee as a detention center. Clark reasoned that if this was done, then the U.S. Attorney General could use his powers to set the "rules" circumscribing the Cubans' conduct and requiring their stay at the Fort until obtaining a sponsor. He concluded that Clinton should not have agreed to the security plan for consolidating the refugees "because there are questions of whether anyone has the authority to detain the refugees."

Clark's opinion created a political crisis for the Clinton Administration and for its relationship with the Cuban-Haitian Task Force responsible for the agreed upon security

58

arrangements. Republican Gubernatorial candidate Frank White accused Clinton of buckling to the federal government; Republican Presidential candidate Ronald Reagan blasted the Administration for mismanagement of the crisis, a popular theme that struck a resonant cord among voters.Clinton aids and the Cuban-Haitian Task Force sought to diminish the negative impact of the Clark opinion. The Governor declared that Cuban-Haitian Task Force member Paul Michel, the U.S. Assistant Attorney General did not think the questions raised by Clark were a "problem" and he promised to get written clarification from Michel. Representative Hammerschmidt said Clark's opinion "was like announcing the score of last year's Cotton Bowl" and repeated Governor Clinton's position that the INS would have detention powers. On September 27, Michel responded to Clark that the refugees' legal status was that of "entrants, status pending" and that they were in the custody of the INS and could not "walk freely out of the resettlement center."

State Attorney General Clark fired back with an announcement that he was prepared to file a lawsuit to force the federal government to clarify the legal status of the refugees. Clark continued to insist that the federal government had not cleared the legal status of the Cubans nor defined the rights and benefits to which they were entitled. On October 9, Clark sent a copy of the proposed suit to Michel addressing the respective powers of the state authorities and the benefit eligibility of the Cubans.[46] This marked a low point in bureaucratic and political infighting over the Marielitos internment and resettlement and conveyed a sense of disarray among the players involved in trying to manage the crisis.

On October 25, U.S. State Attorney Benjamin Civeletti responded officially to Clark's charges clarifying several legal questions that had created the impasse. Civeletti declared that the Cubans were classified as "detainees" under the Federal Immigration and Naturalization Act. According to the Attorney General, this classification gave federal officials power to prevent the Cubans from leaving the camp. He also stated that Cubans settled with sponsors are not permanent residents and are not eligible for state public assistance. Refugee status was available to the Cubans on a case-by-case basis and that refugees would be eligible for state assistance.

Civiletti's response led State Attorney General's Office to withdraw the lawsuit and Clark to declare that local authorities could stop the Cubans leaving the Fort without permission. Clark said that he would make sure that State Human Services Department would know that Cubans were ineligible for benefits and that he would advise them that Cubans applying for Medicaid benefits should be denied. In sum, local authorities fostered the negative stereotype of the Marielitos to deny or restrict benefits and to force federal authorities to adopt the strictest social control measures possible on the population.

Efforts to implement the security agreement were plagued by bureaucratic conflicts and poor coordination among the various agencies involved in the security and resettlement efforts. Significantly, local political and bureaucratic interests responded to the stereotype by fashioning practices banning returnees to the area and arresting others for resettling near the Fort, violating basic civil rights. Problems were evident in the relations between the Security Advisory Council and the Army over the latter's role in camp security; the State Department's officials responsible for refugee resettlement policies and the Voluntary Agencies charged over the status of Cubans with broken sponsorships; the Governor's Office and the Task Force over the consolidation of "mental patients" at the Fort. The goal of maximizing camp security dominated other objectives, such as prompt screening and resettlement and immigrant civil rights. The stress on security supported the immigrants' stigma as pathological.

The consolidation of the Cubans at the Fort was marked by continuing miscommunication and mistrust among the major players. These problems extended from the White House to the local level, those agencies responsible for working with the Cubans on resettlement. On October 11, President Carter campaigning in Florida stated that he had decided to move all the "remaining refugees who have not been settled to Arkansas" and that "Bill Clinton and the Arkansas legislature are cooperating." This announcement caught state officials by surprise and was taken as an indication that the Eidenberg's promise not to send any more Cubans to Arkansas had been broken. This provoked an angry reaction in the state and led Governor Clinton's advisor Robert Lyford to lament "what bothers me is that even if this statement does not mean anything now, it was still made and is causing confusion and we have not been contacted by the White House to help sort out this situation."

Conflicts between bureaucratic agencies' personnel and goals also undermined the basis of the security agreement. A major conflict erupted between the State Department and the Voluntary Agencies involved in resettlement over the matter of Cubans with broken sponsorships. The State Department's Cuban-Haitian Task Force had consented to a policy demanded by Fort Smith Mayor Freeze and City Administrator Lease that all refugees losing sponsors in the area were required to return to the base. This policy was supported by Sheriff Cauthron and State Police Captain Causey and was a quid pro quo for Governor Clinton. There were growing reports of more than a hundred Cubans losing their sponsors and returning to the Fort Smith area. In one case, a town in Florida sponsored a collection drive to return one refugee to Fort Chaffee.

Within days of the consolidation's commencement, it was revealed that voluntary agencies were placing refugees with broken sponsorships into area hotels near the community of Barling. This revelation brought to light deep disagreements over the matter of the Cubans with broken sponsorships. Local authorities complained bitterly in the press and to the Governor, and there were reports of local citizens complaining about the practice. Representatives of the voluntary agencies responded to these criticisms claiming that the return of the Cubans to the Fort was dysfunctional and removed all incentives to make the sponsorship work. Under this policy, Cubans who did not like their sponsors could seek reassignment, thus delaying the resettlement process and creating difficulties in locating additional sponsors.

David Lewis, of the United States Catholic Charities, raised some troubling legal questions over the policy. Lewis challenged the policy's legality asking about the authority to detain Cubans who had obtained legal INS clearances and were therefore within their legal rights to settle in the area. Conflicting organizational objectives between the voluntary agencies advocacy of the Cubans' rights and the State Department's concern with political fallout over "security agreements" was settled by a State Department ruling that the Cubans would be returned and the legal issues referred to the Department of Justice. The voluntary agencies also agreed to use punitive measures including "placing returning Cubans at the bottom of the sponsorship list" as a deterrent to the breaking of sponsorships.

Administrative conflicts also erupted over the matter of the Army's role in providing camp security. The security agreement had established a Security Advisory Council consisting of Cuban-Haitian Task Force representatives and state and local officials to review all matters related to camp security. Eugene Eidenberg had promised that this group would be consulted on all matters related to security and especially to the Army's role in security. On November 6, the Security Advisory Council raised concerns about an announced troop withdrawal protesting the lack of consultation and communication over the nature of the planned withdrawal. This matter brought into focus inter-agency conflicts over the military's role and that of the Security Advisory Council in providing for security. The Council viewed the military's role in the camp as a prophylactic deterrent aimed at the camp interns and as a necessary deployment to assure local residents and contain the political dissatisfaction over the continuing Cuban presence at the Fort.

The military's troop withdrawal announcement also changed the composition of the federal police forces at the camp, replacing Federal Marshals with Federal Protection Service Personnel responsible for guarding federal installations. These revelations led the Security Advisory group on December 4 to call on the Governor to reject the proposed troop withdrawal. The Council advised Clinton that no fewer than 500 troops would be needed (the proposed withdrawal called for a reduction to 150) and that the withdrawal should be phased in over a longer period of time. Senator Bumpers called on the Governor to "countermand" the orders. The Governor responded by calling the proposed action "unacceptable." Military officials responded that the military's presence at the Fort was to assist local police in case they could not cope with the security problem and "there had been no major occurrences that required the use of large army backup forces."[47]

These conflicts pointed to the ongoing difficulties with coordination and led to the direct intervention of the White House's assistant for Inter-Governmental Relations, Eugene Eidenberg. Eidenberg assured the Governor that the administration would be "responsive to the community." Eidenberg's intervention led to a compromise solution to the security dilemma posed by the proposed changes in camp security. On December 7, Colonel Don Karr representing the military at the Fort announced that the Army would begin withdrawing troops but assuring that the troop levels would not drop below 500.

Administrative problems also erupted over the transfer of mentally ill refugees to the Fort. Governor Clinton had insisted during the consolidation talks that mentally ill patients, among whom he wanted included those Cubans with drug related problems, were not transferable to the camp. This position belied the reality that psychologists had considerable disagreement about the mental health of many of the interns. On September 16, an unnamed psychiatrist familiar with the Cubans alleged that 40% of the Cubans at the Fort were "hardcore mental type patients." This allegation was disputed by a psychiatrist screening Cubans at the camp who testified that he found 10 individuals who might need long-term care and another 72 in need of shorter-term therapy.

The Cuban-Haitian Task Force's announcement on November 8 that Cubans with psychiatric problems were being sent to Ft. Chaffee was taken as a breach of faith by state officials. White House spokesperson Eugene Eidenberg denied that the federal government was breaking faith countering that "we are not sending mentally ill refugees to the Chaffee," although admitting that there might be some retarded Cubans included among the transfers. He also noted the case of two women who were suffering from stress and were mistakenly placed in a psychiatric ward as examples of individuals transferred within the scope of the agreement. Eidenberg's statement, however, was contradicted by Justice Department officials who stated that some mentally ill Cubans might be transferred to Chaffee. The conflicting statements led Representative Hammerschmidt to protest, "literally no one knows who is in charge." The controversy was dealt with partially, with the Arkansas Gazette reporting that "some individuals that are mentally ill" would be transferred to the camp.

Bureaucratic conflicts had an unsettling effect on public opinion and heightened political criticism of efforts to deal humanely with the interned Cubans. The negative publicity surrounding the consolidation, not all of which was related to bureaucratic tensions and miscommunication, led to the United States Catholic Charities Director, David Lewis, to ruefully comment that the negative publicity of the camps "was affecting resettlement opportunities because of the reputation (of the Cubans)."

Assessment

The process of stigmatization created profound conflicts over the administration of camp security and over the policies and procedures for screening and resettling the Marielitos. Advocates of tight security measures including Governor Clinton, local politicians, law-enforcement leaders and public opinion pressured for the militarization of the camp and the implementation of exceptional procedures for social control in the camps. Advocates of tougher measures fed the fears created by the stigma. They pressured for tough measures by contributing to the negative stereotypes emphasizing the threatening nature of the Marielitos.

The White House and camp administrators, especially FEMA and the Cuban-Haitian Task Force officials endeavored to offset these pressures and to seek a solution that included security in the context of other goals: the speedy resettlement of Cubans, efficient use of resources, reliance on professionals with broad experience in dealing with refugee populations. In the end, the intense hostility created towards the immigrants and the federal government forced the Carter Administration to appease local reactions by delegating increasing power to determine camp policies and procedures to local forces. The result of this was the transformation of the camp into a prison-like environment that made it increasingly impossible to resettle many of the immigrants.The fears of the Chaffee Cubans helped to affirm the stereotype of the Marielito as pathological and significantly affected the negative entry experience into the U.S. for thousands of Mariel Cubans.

The Marielitos' Rebellion Against Authority at Ft. Chaffee

The Marielitos played an unwitting role in the development of the pathological stereotype, although their participation in this process was reactive and based on their misunderstanding of the powerful political and cultural forces in Cuba and the U.S. that were defining their new identity. The relative powerlessness of the immigrants and the perception that they were being mistreated and labeled, frustrated the detainees at Ft. Chaffee and led the Cubans to adopt strategies to resist their plight. These strategies, some misguided, furthered the pathology stereotype and ultimately defeated the Cubans efforts to change their image.

The Marielitos were forced to participate in constructing their pathological stereotype in Cuba as part of that government's political strategy. Many were forced to confess to crimes of deviance and criminality. Cultural and political misunderstanding or their situation in the U.S. led many to adopt strategies that furthered the negative stereotype in America.

For many Marielitos, the assumption was that being labeled criminal in Cuba and/or having served in prison, would be seen positively in the U.S. Cuban political prisoners were generally well received in the U.S. and the Marielitos expected their experience to be similar. They embraced, and exaggerated their conflicts with Cuban authorities upon arrival in the U.S. This was a serious miscalculation, which led to the pathological label transferring to the U.S.

In addition, the Marielitos brought ingrained attitudes of distrust of public authority and resistance to what they perceived to be unfair and arbitrary rules in Cuba. Many had been involved in the black market. Most were angered at the extensive social controls in Cuba, which regimented their daily lives and rewarded the faithful while punishing those who, like most Marielitos, deviated from the party line. They were, therefore, wary of authority and highly suspicious of bureaucrats whom they distrusted as corrupt and abusive. Resistance to unfair treatment and the perception of pathological was a predictable response to the situation developing in the resettlement camps, such as Ft. Chaffee.

Aguirre, who spent time at the Camp, notes that there was a lack of consistency in the official forms used to process the migrants adding that

> a lack of interagency planning and coordination created difficulties in the planning and readying of an appropriate hardware and software data-processing system and its interface with existing agencies' data management systems. Resettlement processing forms were frequently modified to reflect shifts in the informational needs of the various agencies, and these changes in the forms increased the difficulty of computer operations and of obtaining and locating specific information.[48]

Chaotic camp management, and the size of the population transferred to Chaffee, led to frustrations among Marielitos. By May 14, there were reports of delays in screening of the Cubans due to the shortages of medical supplies, immigration forms, and other necessary supplies. Tensions within the camp grew as the bottlenecks slowed screening and resettlement. Other environmental factors altered the policy-making environment for the Mariel Cubans. Political pressures forced officials to develop new social controls with unanticipated consequences.

A significant number of the Marielitos (between 2-400 hundred) were involved in riots, hunger strikes, and demonstrations at Chaffee. These migrants were labeled as "troublemakers" and "Castro agents" grouped among the dangerous elements that were sent by Cuba to the United States. Cubans participating in protests, demonstrations and uprisings against the perceived unfair and discriminatory treatment also contributed to the stigma.

Table 3

Mariel Resettlement Camps

Camp	Total Population
Eglin	10025
Chaffee	19060
Indiantown-Gap	19094
McCoy	14362
Total	62541

The Marielitos' Perspective

A significant number of the immigrants at Fort Chaffee brought with them experiences and orientations that revealed long-standing rebellion against the political and bureaucratic authority of the Cuban state. These Cubans were used to resisting what they perceived to be an unfair political system in a variety of ways, from direct political activity to economic subversion. For them, resistance to what they perceived as unfair and arbitrary authority was natural, and figuring ways to confront authority was a way of life. These Cubans had resisted becoming part of the established authority system in Cuba, and were seeking to integrate into a new system they did not understand. They had not effectively functioned or experienced a system of political authority within which they could find meaning as citizens.

Furthermore, the Marielitos possessed fewer middle class skills, and many were isolated from families left behind and feared for them. Their distrust of authority and their frustrations created a context for suspicion about their treatment that escalated into different forms of protest.

The Marielitos experiences in Cuba support this view. Many of the émigrés, especially those with some prison experience, lived on the margins of law and society in Cuba. Eighty-one percent of the entrants admitted to having "outside" income other than from their jobs, and 14% volunteered they had extensive experience in the Cuban black market: running illegal repair shops, shoemaking, barbering or selling stolen goods. Typical was Sergio Fernández, a dock worker interviewed by KNJB who regularly siphoned-off merchandise into the black market with the cooperation of the "milicanos" who took the lion's share of the goods. Fernández, and other black marketers, lived in fear of stiff prison terms under the "Ley de la Peligrosidad."

These experiences led to high levels of fear and distrust of those in authority. Cuban authorities were "pincheros" (those who "rip-off" others) and had to manipulate rules to their advantage to survive. The extent of distrust of authority distinguished the Marielito immigrants and presented significant problems to the resettlement agencies. In addition, the immigrants were socially marginal in the sense that they generally did not participate in collective organizations in Cuba. This is unusual in a society that actively promotes mass membership in revolutionary organizations. Most of the immigrants (67%) reported they were not joiners except for laborers who reported compulsory membership.

Significantly, many of the experiences and orientations brought from Cuba were projected by the Marielitos onto their Fort Chaffee experiences. Interviews, transcripts and letters suggest that the Marielitos increasingly saw their Fort Chaffee experience as replicating elements of their Cuban past leading to a propensity to protest and bend the rules as they had done Cuba. One commentator at KNJB made this point:

> I don't want to seem ungrateful to the Americans but the camp is like Cuba, I feel that I am treated unfairly by the officials in power. I believe there is a shortage of goods such as cigarettes and certain foods and some people are making much money selling these goods illegally. To me, this is what I just left.[49]

Incited by family members to protest their treatment, Marielitos, through the limited means available to them, resisted what they believed to be discriminatory and unfair treatment at the hands of political authority. This context set the stage for the social explosions at the Fort.

Signs of discontentment and anger with authority were manifested in KNJB interviews with influential Marielitos. Interviews suggested a current of humiliation at the hands of camp personnel identified with authority in the U.S. Lisa Valladares, a Mariel performance artist interviewed on KNJB, spoke to this in an interview dealing with comments made to the press by an unnamed Army Sergeant (a title the Cubans used indiscriminately to described uniformed authority in the camp) that "Cubans work for anything, even a box of cigarettes." Valladares went on to state that:

> I don't want to be too drastic with this person. But I feel bad. My work here is not for money, but for Cuba and humanity. I didn't come here looking for gum but for liberty for my art. His declaration humiliated me because my work and that of other artists is a human labor...all of us feel bad and humiliated with the statement of the Sergeant.[50]

Feelings of humiliation were aggravated by a sense of powerlessness and lack of a significant role in dealing with internal camp conditions and, especially, social control problems. In a freewheeling transmission including several of the personnel who were asked to assist in running KNJB, Marielitos commented on this fact. Noting the marginalization of the Mariel population, one interviewee stated:

> We need more control over the newspaper and radio information at the Fort. Let's propose to the authorities the goals of the camp information as (a) meeting the information needs of the population (b) educate the masses and inform the American population about the Cuban refugees' conditions...The Americans need to recognize these functions because they need authority to deal with the situation—to identify trouble-makers, find effective leadership, replace troublemakers in positions of leadership...We need to deal with thieves in the stores, dining rooms and to represent the reality of the majori-

ty...Americans' main concern is with social control and we can help in this.[51]

Another of the interviewees doubted that "the Americans" would authorize this adding that:

Let me tell you a personal thing. If we need soap, toothpaste or aftershave lotion at the store we are told that it has already been distributed. This even though there is supposed to be a ration for everyone. We were told that children would receive toys. I found that the toys were being sold on the boulevard, and I saw a sergeant involved in this.[52]

For this interviewee, the perception was that, much as in Cuba, authorities were corrupted and involved in exploitative black market activities. The interviewee's cynical view was that while some Cubans stole and engaged in black market activities, it was the sanction of the authorities which made it possible and they who benefited the most from those activities victimized those who tried to be honest (including children). The notion that the rules of the game were arbitrary and corrupt underpined a great deal of the frustration felt in the camp.

It is interesting to note that another of the interviewees suggested to the panel that they form a delegation to report to the federal police these illicit activities. Others believed that they had to go to the Camp Commander Drummond with these accusations and to offer a "comprehensive solution" to the problems. In the end, the view that authority was too hostile, distant, and uninterested in change prevailed among these discussants, paralleling the prevailing orientations brought from Cuba of authority as "pincheros." For these Cubans, Fort Chaffee became uncomfortably like Cuba.

Interviews with Marielitos still living in the Ft. Smith area confirm that these perceptions were widely held. One interviewee, Ana, a middle-aged women who spent six months at the camp, reported that she was aware of stealing by camp personnel. Ana supported her story by telling about how little meat there was to eat at the camp and the shortages of clothing, which she believes entered as contraband into the

Boulevard economy, as examples. For her, Fort Chaffee with the razor-wire fences, lack of communication, contraband and black marketeering, distant and unresponsive authority, became a metaphor for the prison-like conditions in Cuba.[53]

The Marielitos' experiences and orientations shaped by the Cuban experience set them on a collision course with the U.S. bureaucracy whose perception and expectations of the Marielitos was dramatically different. The conflicts which led to increasingly harsher and punitive bureaucratic measures for social control set off unrest by the migrants and further contributed to their bureaucratic and political construction as agents, trouble-makers, misfits, criminals and pathological. Significantly, these problems escalated after the October consolidation of Marielitos at Fort Chaffee.

The costs to the Marielitos of their conflict with the bureaucracy and of their construction as pathological was mediated by the migrants race, sexual orientation, gender and age. The transformation of the camp into a prison-like atmosphere especially damaged the opportunities for Afro-Cubans, homosexuals and the elderly to find placement opportunities and to begin a new life in the U.S.

Race and the Stigma of Mariels Cubans

The political and bureaucratic conflicts over the Cubans reflected in camp procedures and in the media caused concern among the voluntary agencies responsible for resettlement. The representation of the Cubans at the Fort had a deleterious effect on the morale of the camp interns and intensified feeling of social ostracism toward them. The treatment of the Cubans led to significant frictions between the camp officials and the principal organization involved in the resettlement of the Cubans, the United States Catholic Charities. One cause of the tension arose from the conflict between the demands of the State Department's Cuban-Haitian Task Force (CHTF) that the voluntary agencies expedite the resettlement process for the Cubans and the constant focus on security on the part of the State Department, which conveyed the impression that the camp population posed a threat to civil order.

On November 8 John McCarthy, Director of the USCC Refugee Services, warned that "the longer the Cubans stay in a jail-like atmosphere, the longer it is going to be to resettle them." He warned that the "media attention given to the Cubans has hindered the relocation process."[54] Representatives for the USCC further protested the extraordinary police and security measures being deployed at the camp. Reverend Frank Kennard of the USCC warned, "The high visibility of police was contributing to tensions in the camp." USCC director Lewis added that the camp's atmosphere was repressive and that it was leading to a sense of "resignation of the refugees, which is more of a concern than the violence."

These pressures led Barbara Lawson, the CHTF director at the camp, to launch a public relations campaign to counter the negative reports about Fort Chaffee. Lawson declared that ongoing reports of arson attempts and of violent fights and assaults linked to gangs in the camp were "totally blown out of proportion and have stalled efforts to resettle the refugees." Lawson stated, "Most of the people here deserve to be sponsored out." The CHTF announced that officials would visit 21 cities and mail 40,000 booklets explaining the refugees' situation to the press, churches and Hispanic organizations. This included sponsoring displays of the art work of Marielitos at the Camp, in an attempt to provide a more positive image. The belated efforts to refute the perception of the Cubans did not, however, lead to significant changes in the prison-like atmosphere or to measures meant to improve internal security in the one camp official commented that the State Department's reaction to the problem was to "act as if they ignore it the problem will go away."

Inside the camp, the Cubans' mood varied from anger to resignation, and there was a growing feeling of racial discrimination, which further threatened to undermine the Task Force's efforts to contain the political damage caused by the Mariel crisis. Few security measures were taken to protect the camp interns from the violence being perpetrated by the criminal element. FBI agent William Kell reported, "We do encounter an atmosphere of fear and intimidation among more than six thousand eight-hundred refugees at the camp."

Reports of the population at the Fort indicated that there were individuals and families in the camp being terrorized by gangs. There were reports of women and youths seeking protective custody for fear of their lives. On September 10, sociologist Ben Aguirre, surveying the camp population at the request of the Cuban-Haitian Task Force reported that there were incidents of rape, stabbing and robberies in the camp and that procedures allowed criminals and others accused of crimes to return to the installation where they retaliated against their accusers. He called for measures to protect families, women and juveniles and for the use of force against the criminal minority. Aguirre warned that the press and others should not generalize to the entire camp population from the actions of a criminal minority.[55]

Ironically, as security around the Fort tightened, internal security for the Cubans inside the camp seemed to worsen. One official, Major Phil Turner, of the U.S. Park Service reported that gangs were not all bad because "it means that they feel threatened as individuals and are afraid to operate alone. In some respect that speaks well for the law enforcement officials." For the Major, gang behaviors in the Fort were an expression of the effectiveness of law enforcement, while the interns, regardless of their backgrounds, experienced the effects of the escalating violence.

The criminal element was increasingly concentrated inside the Fort during the period, victimizing the majority, and worsened social tensions in the installation. The Cubans were becoming prison interns in a camp which was primarily directed at containment of the population, but which seemed to ignore the distress of those within its confines. None of the security plans discussed addressed the concern for the increased insecurity of the Marielitos in the camps nor showed awareness that the camp has transformed the immigrants into prisoners.

There were special security areas established for Cubans fearful of the violence, but it was difficult to gain access leading one camp official to comment that one "practically has to have a knife sticking in him." There were reports that Cubans losing sponsorships were routinely placed in level two stockade where those most prone to violence contributing to the punitive character of the camp and resettlement experience were housed.

The CHTF focus on external security and public opinion submerged concerns over resettlement. The CHTF, bound by agreements between the White House and the Governor's Office and by the watchdog role of the Security Advisory group, continued to enforce the security measures developed for the camp. Thousands of Cubans were caught in this dilemma unable to obtain sponsorship while being preyed upon by criminal elements and being stereotyped as delinquents or mentally and physically disabled. Equally disturbing was the growing concentration of Afro-Cubans in the camp. For these Afro-Cubans, there was an additional cost of immigration and internment by virtue of their race. This cost was added to the already high price paid by all the Mariel Cubans by virtue of the political context of their migration experience.

Problems of racial discrimination were brought to light by USCC Director Lewis who stated, "The fact is that we have sponsors who say 'I won't take a black Cuban'" adding that "it hurts but it is a fact." One Cuban intern, Francisco Cabrera Wilson, interviewed outside a recreation center lamented "I go to English classes in the morning and I work in the afternoon. I've had no trouble since I've been here, but I've seen some who have been in trouble leave. In part, I think maybe it is because I'm black." Director Lewis reported that the percentage of blacks at the Fort was increasing. A June 1981 confidential memorandum stated "single black males between the ages of 18 and 55 comprise nearly 95% of the 1,600 migrants. They have few if any skills and little education."[56]

The racial character of the intern population contributed to their social ostracism and to tensions inside the camp. Protests over the placement of some and not others occurred with some frequency at Chaffee and helped to foster the prison-like atmosphere in the camp as well as the arrest of "troublemakers." These problems persisted into 1982 and were part of the disgraceful experience of these immigrants. When Chaffee finally closed and the remaining Cubans were placed in halfway homes or transferred to federal penitentiaries, the Afro-Cuban interns composed the vast majority of the Fort population.

On April 19 and 20 new widespread disturbances once more rocked Fort Chaffee. Tensions at the camp were high following the shooting by a camp policeman of a Cuban attacking another with a machete. The shooting provoked several rock throwing incidents and camp police used tear gas to disperse the angry Cubans. The next day a small protest over another Cuban's detention at the camp stockade for breaking curfew erupted into a confrontation in which forty three security officers and several refugees were injured. The incident led the Security Advisory Group to place on highest alert 500 troops stationed at the U.S. Army base at Fort Polk, Louisiana for fear that the protests would spread among the 2,700 Cubans still held at Fort Chaffee. Unlike the June 1 protest, however, the press and surrounding communities were kept largely uninformed about developments at the camp. Media representatives were allowed to ride through the camp on a military bus and had no access to the Cubans. The event set in motion the final solution to the Cuban "problem" as Governor White renewed his efforts with the Reagan administration to remove the refugees from the base and extracted the promise from the Reagan Administration to have all Cubans removed from the base by August 1981.

The April 1981 protests were met with renewed stereotyping of the Cubans as "antisocial" and set back the efforts initiated by Barbara Lawson to change the public perception of the interns. One staff psychologist was quoted in the *Southwest Times Record* as saying that many of the refugees involved in the riots were "violent and can't get along with people." Cuban-Haitian Task Force Public Affairs Officer Sweeney reiterated the labeling of the Cubans as "sociopaths" claiming "we have a number of people who don't agree with society." Such statements reduced the Cubans' protests over their internment to their "sociopath" and "violent" tendencies reducing their grievances to psychological problems and legitimizing the Administration's decision to terminate the Mariel crisis by unlawfully incarcerating the remaining camp interns in high security federal penitentiaries.

On January 21 the decision was made to move the remaining Cubans permanently to high security prisons in Atlanta and Missouri. With this move, the control over the camp population was moved from the Cuban-Haitian Task Force to the Department of Justice and the goal of eventual resettlement of the Cubans was altered to that of long-term incarceration.

The decision to incarcerate the Cubans was made despite the pending lawsuit by the American Civil Liberties Union challenging the detention of Cubans at the Atlanta facility and also challenging the prison conditions. The move to incarcerate the Cubans met with protests from the Arkansas ACLU. The *Arkansas Democrat* reported Sandra Kurjiaka of the ACLU as saying that the "government must file charges before locking someone up in a penitentiary or military camp or mental hospital." She reported being in shock after visiting Fort Chaffee saying that "it was a concentration camp and I'm not being dramatic."[57]

The Reagan Administration was determined not to repeat the mistakes of the Carter Administration which had cost them a governorship. Democratic Gubernatorial candidate Jim Guy Tucker signaled his plans to make this a campaign issue in the 1982 elections in a campaign speech delivered in Fort Smith. The Cubans' removal from the Fort and their expedient incarceration became a test case of President Reagan's integrity compared to President Carter's. Art Brill of the Justice Department responded to criticisms about the Cubans' incarceration stating, that "President Reagan had made a commitment to move the Cubans out of Fort Chaffee."[58] Similarly, Jim Ciccone, a White House aide, confirmed, "that the main reassurance we are trying to give at this point is that we will meet our commitment to Governor White.

The final episode of the Fort Chaffee experience occurred under a cloak of secrecy and tight security as the Cubans were flown to prisons and metal hospitals in Atlanta, Kentucky and Missouri between January 21 and February 1. The Cubans smuggled out an open letter on January 25 in which they decried their plight and stated, "We are confused and frightened. We came to this country in search of freedom and a chance to work at any menial labor. We have had to wait a long time because we didn't have the family or friends here like the others who came with us. Now we have no voice, we have no defense. Help." The Cubans understood that their status was changing from entrant to detainee to prisoner and resisted within their limited capabilities. One Cuban transported to Missouri refused to sign any papers or surrender civilian clothes at the penitentiary to resist the changed status. Four others who refused to give up their civilian clothes were maced prompting one staff member to state, "the guards had treated the Cubans very aggressively, pulled out the tear gas and hand-cuffed a crippled refugee in a wheelchair."

Labeled as "sociopaths" and "violent" the Cubans' final plea did not elicit much sympathy or support for their plight. The tragic conclusion to the Cubans' camp internment met with lit-tle empathy. Senator Dale Bumpers was quoted in the *Arkansas Gazette* as saying that he "hoped that there is legit-imate reason for the transfer" and that "he hoped we were not betraying our ethics." The *Gazette* lambasted White saying that "he will not easily rid the shame of exploiting these luck-less refugees from communism" and ruefully commenting "not even the courts can dispel the disgrace at the hands of our own politicians."

More in keeping with the hostile reception of the Cubans at Fort Chaffee, as the last of the Cubans were transplanted to federal penitentiaries, Governor White commented that he was glad to see the refugees go and that "sending most of the Cubans to prisons did not concern him." In the end, he said, Fort Chaffee was already a prison and not much different from the federal penitentiary at Atlanta. The stigma of these Cubans as undesirable allowed the Reagan Administration to deprive these Cubans of their freedom without due process.

An Assessment

The Marielitos experiences in the camps were profoundly disorienting. Camp experiences profoundly changed their identity as refugees fleeing communism. These conditions help to explain the significantly higher rates of mental disor-ders found among the refugees, the self-destructive behaviors of many of the camp interns, and the post-camp adaptation experiences. The confluence of stereotyping in Cuba and the U.S., the negative experiences suffered by many in Cuba, and the subsequent camp experiences in the U.S. contributed to the enormous costs of migration for the Marielitos.

The subsequent prolonged internment in refugee camps undoubtedly affected the entrants ability to become self-sufficient in a short period of time. It appears that the probability of maladaptation increases if the period between the initial migration and the final resettlement is longer than a few weeks or months. The situation can be attributed to the stressful living conditions inside the resettlement centers.

Feelings of hopelessness and powerlessness, led a few Marielitos to act in destructive ways in the camps contributing to a perception of their difference and to the stigma. According to official reports, there were numerous fistfights at the camp as well as more serious incidents of violence. Using a Ft. Chaffee chronology from May of 1980 to February of 1981, which details incidents of violence, there were fourteen aggravated assaults and stabbings, eight cases of arson, and one burglary committed by an escaped Cuban in the Fort Smith area. These figures must be read carefully and fail to account for numerous cases of violence that went unreported or did not result in prosecution, including rapes, intimidation and other forms of aggression.

By June of 1981, a CHTF confidential memoranda indicated that "staff work is noisy, crowded and high tension... last week only ten persons left to deal with the CHTF caseload causing more demands and unruliness." The memo warned that in "the heat of the summer a human tragedy can be anticipated, the Cubans will be the victims." This memorandum implicitly acknowledged the terrible cost of the pathological stereotype to innocent Marielitos.

The pathological stereotype had profound implications for the adaptation experiences of the refugees.

The Adaptation Experiences of the Marielitos and the "Costs"of the Stereotype

There is a growing body of research on the social and economic adaptation of the Mariel Cubans in the United States. Research has been impeded by the understandable reluctance of the Marielitos to self-identify due to their migratory experiences and the negative stereotypes of the group. Boswell,

Rivero and Díaz in their study optimistically conclude that "despite the reputation created by both the American and Cuban presses, the vast majority of Mariel refugees are quickly and effectively accommodating to life in the United States."[59] The authors attribute this to large-scale financial and social assistance provided by the Cuban-American population that arrived prior to the Mariel wave.

Empirical research on the adaptation experiences of this immigrant wave conducted by Portes, Clark and Manning shows a more difficult period of early adaptation marked by frequent bouts of enforced unemployment, low-paid work, and dependence on welfare and charity. The most dramatic difference between the Mariel group and earlier arrivals is found to be in their employment levels. After three years, the Marielitos' male unemployment more than doubled that of the Cuban refugees during the 1970's, while among women the unemployment rate was close to 60%. The study found that "two-thirds of unemployed respondents were looking for work at the time of the survey. Hence the rate of involuntary unemployment...amounts to 27%, a figure three times greater than among the Cuban-born population in 1980." Table 4 details some of the differences in labor market outcomes among the immigrants.[60]

Labor Market Outcomes by Selected Predictor Variables

Predictor	Category	Number	Unemployed percent	Welfare percent (triman score)	Occupation Status	Current Income 1979 p/month
Race	non-white	64	50	40.6	26.1	673
	white	458	39.8	27.1	36	812
	p<		0.09	0.03		0.86
Help from						
Kin	little-0	270	49.6	36.3	34.5	753
Upon Arrival	fair amount	274	29.9	20.5	37.2	835
	or more					
p.c.	p.c.		0.001	0.001	0.001	0.07

Significantly, the study finds that single and younger respondents as well as non-whites are significantly less likely to have been employed in 1983-84, and that those immigrants with at least one relative in the U.S. at the time of arrival are more likely to have found paid work. The authors conclude that employment in the U.S. was more linked to the social networks of the arrivals than to any ascriptive characteristics. Not surprisingly, the Marielitos on the whole had fewer family and social networks of support than earlier exiles, a condition that the authors find to be strongly correlated with occupational status and income in the new society. While the Mariel group's educational attainment in Cuba was comparable to that of émigrés of the 1970's, their backgrounds did not provide an effective gateway into the labor market. Consequently, the Mariel Cubans have tended to concentrate in the informal labor market and self-employment, areas that are less well compensated.

Mariel Cubans tended to express comparable levels of satisfaction with their new society when compared with the earlier Cuban immigrants and voiced similar plans to acquire citizenship. Significantly, three-fourths of those surveyed by the study reported experiences with discrimination from the pre-1980 Cuban community. The authors note that while Cubans are not the first immigrant group to suffer "fractures" of internal solidarity due to the arrival of a new wave of "different" arrivals, concludes that it is to be determined whether the Cuban community can effectively rise to the challenge of supporting, rather than hindering, the incorporation experience of the more recent newcomers.

The Aguirre, Sáenz and Sinclair-James study of census data on 50,958 people of Cuban origin found a significant impact of the role of government programs and procedures on the institutionalization of the immigrants.[61] This study finds that the Mariel Cubans behavior did not differ significantly from earlier Cuban immigrants. Reinforcing the argument made by M. Hamm, the study finds that what was different about this migration was the role of "moral entrepreneurs," government officials who enforce new "deviance-creating" programs.

According to this study, "the Marielitos were the first sizeable group of Cuban immigrants to have direct experience with INS personnel and operations. The use of the INS during the Mariel crisis, the "entrant" labeling of the new immigrants which deprived them of refugee status, and their detention in military camps throughout the country were the structural preconditions for the moral redefinition which justified hostility against them and fueled the moral epidemic." Aguirre et. al. thus locate a significant degree of responsibility for the prejudice experienced by the immigrants in the labor market and in their social adaptation experiences on these policies and their effectiveness in redefining the migration's significance.

Ten years after their arrival in the U.S. the authors found that the Marielitos stigmatization continued to affect their adaptation experiences. For example, the study found that in 1990, 23% of the sample were looking for work and 27% were living in poverty. They tended to hold jobs that paid lower salaries, suggesting that their labor market participation had not changed significantly from the early 1980's and corroborating the findings of the Portes et. al. study. Significantly, the study found that holding constant education, race, income, English ability, and family status that "being a Marielito increases the rate of imprisonment more than twice." When the authors disaggregate the category Mariel by race, age and gender they find that being black increases the chances of incarceration more than double, while similar patterns hold for youth and women. This far exceeds the norm for earlier Cubans, which the authors suggest, is related to the virulent effect of "Mariel" stigma.

Special Populations: Gays, Minors and Disabled

Reports of large numbers of homosexuals among the Marielitos and stories of alleged homosexual abuses especially of minors in the resettlement camps built the pathological construction of the émigrés. Reports that as many as 20,000 homosexuals came via Mariel were frequently contradicted by gay groups, and social service personnel. Gay advocates who visited the camps found that less than 6% of the immigrants at Fort McCoy, and less than 1% of those at Fort Chaffee were gay. Siro del Castillo, Director of the Krome resettlement camp estimated even fewer, claiming that less than 100 of the 50,000 processed at the camp were homosexuals.[62] Ambiguous and ambivalent information about this reported behavior was frequently presented in a negative light as part of the news spectacle. This alleged practice forged an environment of public uncertainty that fed into the process of deviance construction.

The practice of exaggerating the alleged moral deviance of the Marielitos, which was associated with homosexuality, supports the arguments about "moral entrepreneurs" and leading a "moral crusade" aimed at this wave of immigrants.[63] The systematic exaggeration of homosexuality among the Cubans coupled with the emphasis on the sexual threat posed to the society served to intensify antagonism towards new immigrants in general and the Cubans in particular. It justified demands for intensified immigrant control measures, such as expanded prisons, border patrol personnel, and detention centers.

The press also amplified the image of immigrants' threat related to sexual orientation. Homosexuals, were often portrayed as threatening rape against minors. The *Arkansas Gazette*'s August 1, 1980 report, for example, claimed that "some people are in protective custody who fear for their lives in the camps and there have been incidents in which young males have asked for custody from homosexuals."[64] The images of the Marielito homosexual as a danger to society is one of the most enduring images of the émigrés.

The extent of this threat was amplified by accounts such as the *Washington Post*'s report alleging that "up to 20,000 homosexuals could be part of the refugee wave that arrived in this country during the 'Freedom Flotilla', although the exact figures are hard to determine." Quoting Bill Traugh, FEMA's Director at Fort Chaffee, the Post adds that "it has been impossible to determine the reason why there are so many homosexuals among the refugees...we have discussed this matter several times with staff and we have not arrived at a satisfactory answer."[65]

The mentally ill population in the migration was small, but also had a disproportionate impact on the representation of the exodus. Data by Harmon and others suggest that some of the Cubans "had lengthy histories of psychiatric treatment in Cuba, including contacts which began as early as childhood and adolescence, attempted suicides, and hospitalization with electroconvulsive therapy."[66] The mentally ill charged with criminal conduct (which ranged from attempted murder to public lewdness, petty larceny and possession of a weapon) received unusually severe penalties, supporting the macro analysis of Aguirre. While there is little doubt that the Cuban regime sought to "poison" the image of the migrants by deporting mentally ill Cubans, the authors conclude that, for their sample of 54, the experience at arrival in the U.S. with "physical hardship, emotional tension, economic difficulties, and restriction of freedoms" encouraged the reversion to such behaviors.

Stigmatization entailed high costs. To the Marielitos, the costs were distributed disproportionately by race, education, gender and age. For many less educated, younger Afro-Cubans the cost of this reception was in prolonged camp internment. These immigrants' experience with prolonged detention, cultural disorientation in military camps, unrealized expectations about American society, and rejection by even the ethnic community, contributed to higher rates of mental disorder such as depression, alcoholism, and drug abuse.

Conclusions

The stigmatization of the Marielitos in two societies of radically divergent ideologies and political systems seems paradoxical. The history of Cuban migration contradicted the likelihood of such a phenomenon. Indeed, the pattern was those the Cuban regime stereotyped as "worms" or traitors were cleansed in the U.S., almost uncritically. A Cuban stigma had little currency in the U.S., and vice versa. The dissidents and freedom fighters of South Florida became in translation the lumpens of Cuban society.

Research strongly supports the conclusion that political factors in Cuba and in the U.S. led to the Marielitos' stigmatization as pathological. There were some remarkable similarities in the process of stigmatization in both the U.S. and Cuba. The reasons for the synchronization of stigma in both countries have different causes in both societies; yet in both the process of stigmatization bore resemblances. First, the role of "political entrepreneurs" was critical in both societies in creating, disseminating and benefiting from the stereotype's persistence. In both countries, political entrepreneurs linked to organized interest groups played a crucial role in the process. Cuban mass organizations, such as the CDR's, rank and file party members and workers were mobilized in a cultural and political attack on the Marielitos. The stereotype functioned to benefit the entrepreneurs by building social cohesion and support for political goals: the legitimacy of the revolution in Cuba and for political leaders and agencies supervising the Marielitos in the United States.

In the U.S., the stereotype functioned to support the goals of leaders linked to organized interest groups opposed to the migrants. Stereotyping functioned to displace anger over economic problems, racial tensions surrounding the differential treatment of Cubans and Haitian immigrants, and jealousies and frustrations of Latino groups towards the Cubans. The immigrants became a lighting rod for social frustrations in the U.S. In both societies, the Marielitos found little political support for their aspirations.

In both countries, government elites adopted deviance creation. In Cuba, political leaders such as Castro played a key role in the process. There, elites also used bureaucratic organizations and political agencies, such as the CDR's , in labeling the refugees as pathological. Marielitos in Cuba adopted the labels of deviant, criminal etc, in the process of obtaining a right to passage out of the island. In the U.S., the process of stigmatization functioned more at the level of bureaucratic agencies competing for resources and public support based on their role in protecting society from these new immigrants. Both countries experienced a practice of political witch hunting. In the U.S. that process in the 1980's added to the high levels incarceration and economic marginality of Marielitos. Accounts also emphasize the role of race and class in the process, conditions which when added to the politically inspired discrimination, canceled the human capital resources that the group as a whole brought to the U.S.

The role of "moral entrepreneurs" in the U.S. and Cuba in the process of stigmatization is especially interesting. In Cuba, key political elites, including President Castro, pursued political goals by stigmatizing the émegrés as pathological. There is scarce evidence of how local elites in Cuba might have benefited from this process. In the U.S. the work of Aguirre et al. and Hamm on the political and economic functions of the moral crusade against the Marielitos suggest that there were political and economic motivations behind the stigmatization and that these entrepreneurs were successful in distorting the facts about this group.

Studies suggest that a moral crusade was launched against the Marielitos by the INS and the Justice Department, reaching its height in the late 1980's. INS crusaders employed an array of threatening images, factual distortions and symbolic references to create a specific image of Mariel Cubans. The official approach used by the INS during the latter half of the 1980's was to exaggerate the criminal propensity of those Marielitos already in custody, thereby justifying the continued criminalization of hundreds.

Mark Hamm links the moral crusade against Marielitos to political problems of Attorney General Edwin Meese and to the efforts of the INS to use the Mariel stereotype to gain increased agency budgets:

> The INS capitalized on this status in the political arena to further enhance its own importance. In terms of public exposure and political recognition, it is in fact safe to conclude that the Marielitos were the best thing that ever happened to the INS. Before the Freedom Flotilla, the INS was a relatively obscure subdivision of the Justice Department that operated on a yearly budget of roughly $900 million. In 1983, the INS broke the billion-dollar mark with a budget of $1.07 billion. Then came the moral crusade and with it the most exorbitant budgets in the history of the INS, more than 100% increase in six years.[67]

The pattern of incarceration of Mariel Cubans further supports this view. The INS evidence that a small minority estimated at 1,306 aliens had "questionable" backgrounds and claims of crime waves caused by the Marielitos were submerged by the pathological stereotype. W. Willbank's study of crime rates in Miami, for example, found that:

> A great deal of attention has been given in the media to the involvement. In homicide (as victims and offenders) of the Cuban Mariel refugees. At least 42 homicide victims in 1980 were from the Mariel Boatlift. Since the refugees were only in Dade County half of 1980, their victimization rate would be approximately 84 per 1000, a rate approximately equal to that for blacks in the county. And if one controlled for the disproportionate number of males and young adults, the rate would be below that of blacks in Dade county. Calculations suggest that the Marielitos were responsible for only 25% of the 60% increase in homicide victimization.[68]

To be certain, there were significant differences in the processes for creating the stigma. In Cuba, for example, the process was consistent with the regime's character, centralized and top-down. There, the state, and the highest level leadership took the initiative to frame the stigma with strategic deliberation. Once the stigmatization policy was defined, the processes flowed from top to bottom with the media, neighborhood committees, party activists, workers involved in the process. Public opinion was mobilized and a concerted campaign to disseminate the stigma developed. This campaign included the infiltration of hard-core criminal elements into the mix of migrants, but more significantly, using state procedures—(bureaucratic organizations, people's courts)— to make stigmatization a necessary condition for departure for many émegrés. The policy was successful in disseminating the stigma among the refugees and creating a context in which the Marielitos unwittingly collaborated in their own negative stereotyping. Clearly, without the Cuban government's role in creating the stigma, the negative stereotype would not likely have affected the fate of this group in the U.S. This must weigh heavily in the assessment of responsibility for stigmatization of this group.

In the U.S., the process was characterized by competition among local and national political elites and bureaucracies. Despite early efforts to cleanse the Cuban stigma with Cold War categories, the Carter Administration soon realized the political risks of the "open hearts" policy and retreated to a policy of managing fallout from the Marielitos. Under the circumstances, a process of competition was set forth by local and national political elites in which the rules of the game seemed to be to maximize the threat of the refugees, blame the problem on another level of government or bureaucracy and to claim the role of protecting the community by advocating ever harsher controls over the migrants. The stigma benefited those interests whose operational budgets depended on having a large-scale threat perception fueled by mass fear of the migrants and by political elites competing to appear as most concerned with public safety and able to portray opponents as insensitive to the public interest in personal security.

The mass media also contributed to the process of stereotyping in both countries. In Cuba, the media's role was to voice the official government line on the social pathology of the Marielitos. In the U.S., the mass media reinforced the negative stereotypes of the cubans. In Cuba, the media adapted the regime's terms of lumpen, delinquent, criminal to characterize the group as a whole. In the U.S. the media similarly adopted generic terms and amplified them in describing the émegrés; such as criminal, socio-paths, gang members, brutalized and brutalizing.

Twenty years later, many Mariel Cubans have successfully adapted to the U.S. and have contributed to the arts, business, society and education. These migrants have overcome the stigma and have disproved the negative stereotypes. Despite this, for many others, the costs of the stigmatization remain very high and adaptation elusive in the face of depression, incarceration and distrust of authority. Levels of unemployment and reported discrimination by others, including other Cuban-Americans, are high. Time will likely obliterate the worst of the Mariel stereotype, but in the meantime, the human costs of a highly politicized migration demand that states desist from using innocent people as instruments of conflict. For civilized nations, the Mariel experience and its aftermath should serve as a wake up call concerning the need to depoliticize migrations and to deal with the human and social costs of immigration free from racial, ethnic or ideological stereotypes.

The bibliography, which follows, should prove to be of use to scholars who are interested in pursuing research in the field of immigration studies related to the Mariel experience. The large volume of scholarly work on this topic is organized to assist researchers in referencing different critical topics that have been the focus of scholarly work in this field and which point them in new directions. I hope that the bibliography will further additional lines of inquiry, such as the extent to which the Mariel stigma is passed down from one generation to the next. Twenty years after the exodus, there are many important questions remain concerning the immigration experience of the Mariel population and their stigmatization.

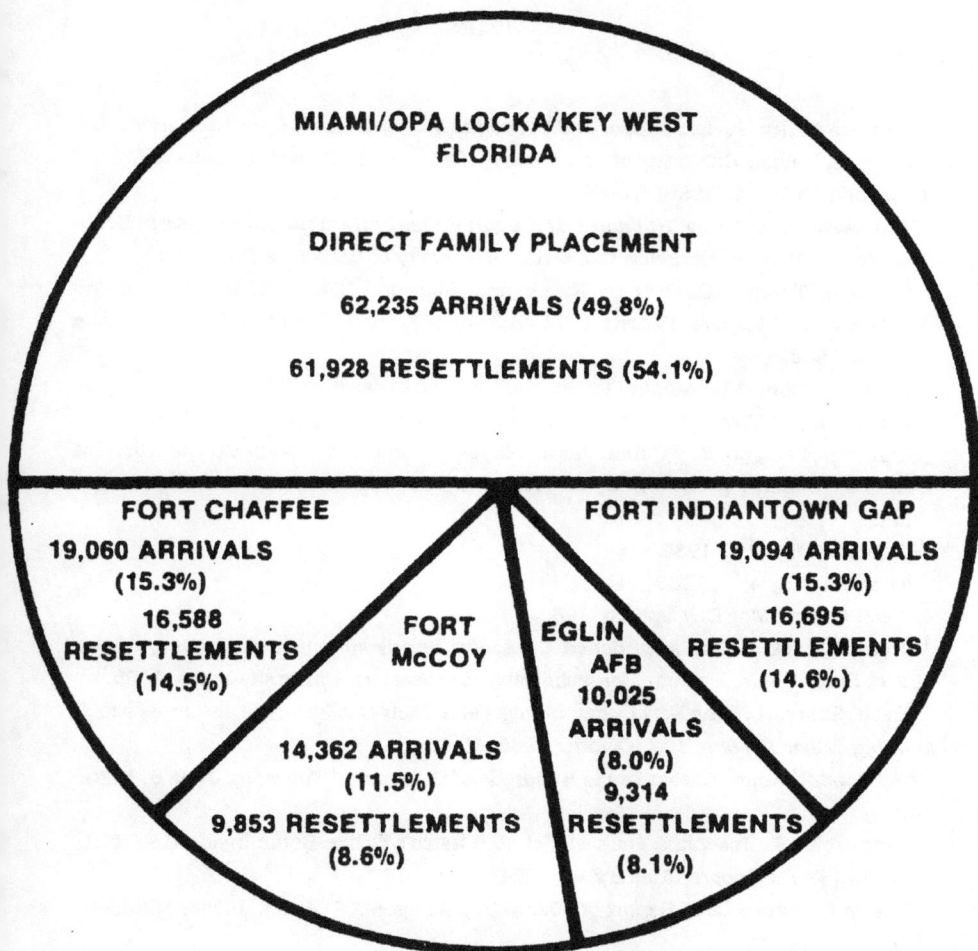

MIAMI/OPA LOCKA/KEY WEST FLORIDA

DIRECT FAMILY PLACEMENT

62,235 ARRIVALS (49.8%)

61,928 RESETTLEMENTS (54.1%)

FORT CHAFFEE
19,060 ARRIVALS (15.3%)
16,588 RESETTLEMENTS (14.5%)

FORT McCOY
14,362 ARRIVALS (11.5%)
9,853 RESETTLEMENTS (8.6%)

EGLIN AFB
10,025 ARRIVALS (8.0%)
9,314 RESETTLEMENTS (8.1%)

FORT INDIANTOWN GAP
19,094 ARRIVALS (15.3%)
16,695 RESETTLEMENTS (14.6%)

Cuban processing and resettlement by facility
(By percent of total arrivals and percent of total resettlement)

(Source: US Department of State, Cuban-Haitian Task Force,
A Report of the Cuban-Haitian Task Force, 1 December 1980, p. 75.)

[1]Pedraza-Bailey, Silvia. *Political and Economic Immigrants in America: Cubans and Mexicans.* Austin: University of Texas Press, 1985. [2]Bach, Robert L. "Cuba in Crisis," *Migration Today,* 8 (1980) :15-18.

[3]García, María Cristina. *Havana USA:Cuban Exiles and Cuban Americans in South Florida, 1959-1994.* Berkeley, California.: University of California Press,1996.

[4]Boswell, Thomas D., Manuel Rivero and Guarioné Díaz. *Bibliography for the Martel-Cuban Diaspora.* Paper no. 7. University of Florida: Center for Latin American Studies, 1988.

[5]Boswell, Thomas D., Manuel Rivero and Guarioné Díaz. Op. Cit.

[6]Jeff Lyons, "If This is Slavery, Cubans Want More of it," Friday, May 2, 1980: 1.

[7]Aguirre, Benigno E. "Cuban Mass Migration and the Social Construction of Deviants," *Bulletin of Latin American Research,* 13 (1994): 155-83.

[8]*Ibid.*

[9]Granma, May 4th , 1980

[10]Granma, May 4th , 1980

[11]Fidel Castro, May Day Speech, 1980.

[12]Hamm, Mark S. *The Abandoned Ones: the Imprisonment and Uprising of the Martel Boat People.* Boston, Massachusetts: Northeastern University Press, 1995.

[13]Bach, Robert. L. "The New Cuban Immigrants: Their Backgrounds and Prospects," *Monthly Labor Review, 103* (October 1980):39-46.

[14]"As Boatlift Wanes, Castro Sends Hundreds of Criminals," Thursday, June 5, 1980: 1A.

[15]Lang, John S., Joseph L. Galloway, et al. "Castro's Crime Bomb Inside U.S." *U.S. News and World Report,* January 16, 1984: 16:27.

[16]"Camp Personnel Deny Report of 20,000 Gay Refugees," Tuesday, July 8, 1980:1A.

[17]Aguirre, *Op. Cit.*

[18]Rivera, Mario A. *Decision and Structure: U.S. Refugee Policy in the Martel Crisis.* Lanham, Md:University of Maryland Press, 1991

[19]Miami Herald, June 12, 1980.

[20]Miami Herald, June 17, 1980

[21]Engstrom

[22]Kuzban, Ira. " A Critical Analysis of Refugee Law," 36 U. *Miami Law Review.* 865 (1986).

[23]Ibid

[24]Engstrom, David W. *Decision Making Adrift: The Carter Administration and the Martel Boatlift.* New York, New York: Rowman Littlefield Publishers, 1997.

[25]"Alexander Urges U.S. To Detain Refugees," May 13, 1980: 1A

[26]"Alexander Urges U.S. To Detain Refugees," May 13, 1980: 1A

[27]"Refugees to Arrive In Arkansas Today; Fort Chaffee Readied," May 9, 1980: p. 1A

[28]Health of Cuban Refugees Deteriorating, Doctors Say," May 1, 1980

[29]Silver, Larry B., Et al. "The Cuban Immigration of 1980," *Public Health Reports*, (January-February, 1981): 100:40-8.

[30]"Alexander Urges U.S. To Detain Refugees," May 13, 1980: 1A

[31]"Will Arrest Cubans, Community Officials Near Chaffee Warn," May 29, 1980: p. 1A

[32]The New Policy on Refugees," May 17, 1980: 12A

[33]"15 Members of Klan Hold Protest At Fort Smith Against Refugee," May 25, 1980: 1A

[34]Thousands Riot at Fort Chaffee, 15 Troopers, 4 Refugees Injured," June 2, 1980: p. 1A

[35]"Fort Security Improved, State Police To Stay, Clinton Says," June 7, 1980: 2A

[36]Fellone, Franf. "Clinton Supports Shootings," June 7, 1980: Front Page.

[37]"Chaffee Policy Changed, Refugees Must Have Clearances to Leave," June 10, 1980: 1A

[38]"Use of Fort Rest of '80 Is Asked," July [26], 1980: p.1A

[39]"Police Express Concern For Security at Chaffee, Riot Control Promised," August 6, 1980: 3A

[40]"Carter's Aide Apologizes, But Says Cubans Due Soon," August 6, 1980: 1A

[41]"Carter Promises to Consult Clinton," August 5, 1980: 1A

[42]"Demands by Clinton On Chaffee Security Had Been Met Earlier," September 12, 1980: 1A

[43]"More Detailed Response Needed On Security Proposal, Clinton Says," September 19, 1980: 6A

[44]*Ibid.*

[45]"Arrests of Refugees Illegal, Clark Declares," September 26, 1980: 1A

[46]"Clark Delays Suit on Status Of Refugees," October 15, 1980: 12A

[47]"Troop Reduction at Chaffee 'Unacceptable,' Clinton Says; Delay, Limits Urged," December 4, 1980: p.8A

[48]Aguirre, *Op. Cit.*

[49]KNJB audio tape 1. University of Arkansas Library, Fayetteville, Arkansas.

[50]*Ibid.*

[51]KNJB audio tape 3. University of Arkansas, Library, Fayetteville, Arkansas

[52]*Ibid.*

[53]Interview conducted in Ft. Smith, Arkansas on June 22, 1996.

[54]Cubans Left at Chaffee Developing Mood of Resignation," November 21, 1980: 8A

[55]Aguirre, *Op. Cit.*

[56]Lindsey, Robert. "U.S. is Finding That No One Wants to Accept Last Cuban Refugess," Sunday August 9, 1981:26A.

[57]Speed, Kay. "Cubans Face Longer Stay in Prison," January 21, 1982: Front Page.

[58]Taylor, Stuart, Jr. "Reagan's Move to Control Immigration," November 4, 1981:21a.

[59]Boswell et. al. *Op.Cit.* p.5.

[60]Portes, Alejandro, Juan M. Clark, and Robert D. Manning. "After Mariel: a Survey of the Resettlement Experiences of 1980 Cuban Refugees in Miami," *Cuban Studies/Estudios Cubanos,* 15, (Summer 1985): 37-59

[61]Aguirre, Benigno E. Rogelio Sáenz, and Brian Sinclair James. "Marielitos Ten Years Later: The Scarface Legacy," *Social Science Quarterly,* 1998

[62]Camp Personnel Deny Report of 20,000 Gay Refugees," Tuesday, July 8, 1980:1A.

[63]Aguirre (1998), *Op.cit.* and Hamm (1995), *Op. Cit.*

[64]"Protection Sought For Cubans," August 1, 1980: p.1A

[65]Brown, Warren. "Cuban Boatlift Drew Thousands of Homosexuals," July 7, 1980:1A.

[66]Harmon R.B, R. Rosner, and M. Wiederlight. "The Mariel Refugee and the New York Criminal Court," *New York City Dept. Of Mental Health,*:32, No.3 (1987): 725-735

[67]*Ibid.*

[68]Willbanks, Williams. *Murder in Miami: An Analysis of Homicide Patterns and Trends in Dade County (Miami) Florida, 1917-1983.* Lanham, Maryland: University Press of America, 1984.

Descriptions
of the
Photographs
Taken
at Ft. Chaffee

1.   Photo shows three Marielitos waving a American flag. This was typical of the early days at Ft. Chaffee when grateful Marielitos sought to embrace symbols of American freedom.

2. A group of Marielitos standing on the other side of a rope that divided the camp between areas for Marielitos and other personnel. The rope represented a barrier beyond which lies freedom.

3. Ft. Chaffee before the chain link fences and security measures implemented following the June uprisings.

4. Life at Ft. Chaffee revolved around sports.

5. Ibid

6. Among the most popular activities at the Fort was playing dominos, a traditional Cuban pass time

7.A large number of Marielitos were Afro-Cubans who brought with them
traditions rooted in the African heritage. Here a group is celebrating an African ritual
dance led by an Afro-Cuban priest or "Santero" dressed in white.

8.A Mariel woman performing a ceremonial dance based on Yoruba traditions.
Among the Yoruba, Gelede represents the process of celebrating the power of the
Ancient Mothers to ensure the continuation of family lines. Gelede often appears in
the form of dance masquerades that give way to activating the power of Iron [Yoruba
word] meaning vision.

98

9.Many children lived at Ft.Chaffee with their families. This photo shows recreational pass times for children at the Fort.

10.A child watching a baseball game, another favorite pass time.

11. Cuban sports fanaticism for boxing is renowned. Several boxers joined the Mariel migration, and here a boxing match is featured.

12. As tensions increased, the police and military presence at the camp took on a visible and intimidating presence. This photo shows a typical amassing of strength by Ft Chaffee authorities in response to Marielitos protests.

13. A group of military personnel at Ft. Chaffee. These Puerto Rican National Guard served a stint maintaining security at the camp.

14. A major concern in the post camp consolidation period was the supposed violent nature of the Marielitos. The photo shows confiscated weapons seized during a search of the population. Among the items are knives, rules, masking tape and paint brushes.

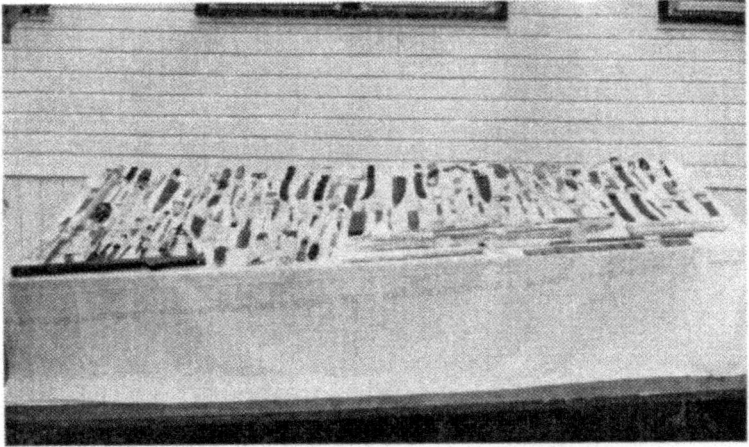

15. This photo shows a more carefully presented array of weapons including knives and screwdrivers.

16. Mariels migrants were encouraged to paint to express their feelings. Here an exhibit of Mariel art is being viewed by Chaffee staff

17. Afro-Cuban Marielitos, especially women, were among the most difficult to place with sponsors. Among the later placements, pregnancies were common.

18. Governor White of Arkansas visited the camp to discuss the fate of the remaining migrants.

A Research
Bibliography

Books, Book Chapters and Monographs

1.   Adams, Michael R., and Raymond Fullerton. "The Cuban Exodus Revisited." *U.S. Naval Institute Proceedings,* August 1981.

2. Alegría, Fernando, and Jorge Ruffinelli, eds. *Paradise Lost or Gained? The Literature of Hispanic Exile*. Houston, Texas: Arte. 3. Publico Press, 1990.

3. Aleinikoff, Thomas Alexander, and David A. Martin. *Immigration: Process and Policy*. St. Paul, Minnesota: West Publishing Company, 1985.

4. Almendros, Néstor. *A Man with a Camera*. Translated by Rachel Phillips Belash. New York, New York: Farrar, Straus & Giroux, 1984.

5. Arenas, Reinaldo. *Necesidad de libertad: Mariel: Testimonios de un intelectual disidente*. México: Kosmos Editorial S.A., 1986.

6. Ascher, Carol. "The United States'New Refugees: A Review of the Research on Resettlement of Indochinese, Cubans, and Haitians," *Urban Diversity Series*, no. 75. New York, New York: Columbia University, Institute for Urban and Minority Education, November 1983.

7. Ascher, Carol, and Darryl Alladice. "Refugees in the United States. A Bibliography of ERIC Documents," *ERIC/CUE Bibliography,* no.7. New York, New York.: Columbia University, Institute for Urban and Minority Education, April 1982.

8.   Bach, Robert L. "The Cuban Exodus: Political and Economic Motivations" In *Caribbean Exodus*, edited by Barry B. Levine, 87-136. New York: Praeger Publishers, 1987.

9.   Bach, Robert L. "The Freedom Flotilla Cuban Immigrants," In *Immigrants and Refugees: The Caribbean and South Florida*, edited by Mark Rosenberg. Dialogue Series no. 2. Miami, Florida: Florida International University, Latin American and Caribbean Center, March 1981.

10. Bean, Frank and Marta Tienda. *The Hispanic Population of the U.S.* New York: Russell Sage Foundation, 1987.

11. Beruvides, Esteban M. *Cuba: Anuario histórico 1991*. Miami, Florida: Adventures International,1992.

12. Borjas, George J. *Friends or Strangers: The Impact of Immigrants on the U.S. Economy*. New York, New York: Basic Books Inc.,Publishers, 1990.

13. Boswell, Thomas D., and James R. Curtis. *The Cuban-American Experience: Culture, Images, And Perspectives*. Totowa, New Jersey: Rowan and Allanheld Publishers, 1983.

14. Boswell, Thomas D. and Emily Skop. *Hispanic National Groups in Metropolitan Miami*. Miami: Cuban American Policy Center, Cuban American National Council, 1995.

15. Boswell, Thomas D., Manuel Rivero, and Guarioné Díaz, eds. *Bibliography for the Mariel-Cuban Diáspora*. Paper no.7 Gainsville, Florida: University of Florida Center for Latin American Studies, 1988.

16. Boswell, Thomas D. "Cuban- Americans," In *Ethnicity in Contemporary America*, edited by Jesse O. McKee. Dubuque, Iowa: Kendall-Hunt Publishing Company, 1984.

17. Bretos, Miguel. *Cuba & Florida: Exploration of an Historic Connection, 1539-1991*. Miami: The Historical Association of Southern Florida, 1991.

18. Camayd-Freixas, Yohel. *Crisis in Miami: Community Context and Institutional Response in The Adaptation of 1980 Boatlift Cubans and Undocumented Haitians Entrants in South Florida*. Boston, Massachussets: Boston Urban Research & Development Group, 1988.

19. Carbonell, Néstor T. *And the Russians Stayed: The Sovietization of Cuba*. New York, New York.: William Morrow and Co.,1989.

20. Carter, Jimmy. *Keeping Faith*. New York: Bantam Books, 1982.

21. Castro, Max J. "The Politics of Language in Miami," In *Miami Now! Immigration, Ethnicity and Social Change*, edited by Guillermo J. Grenier and Alex Stepick. Gainesville, Florida: University of Florida Press, 1992.

22. Clark, Juan M., José I. Lasaga, and Rose S. Roque. *The 1980 Mariel Exodus: An Assesment and Prospect*.

Washington D.C.: Council for Inter-American Security, 1981.

23. Copeland, Ronald, and Patricia Weiss-Fagan. *Political Asylum: A Background Paper on Concepts, Procedures and Problems.* Washington D.C.: Refuge Policy Group, 1982.

24. Coser, Lewis A. *Refugees Scholars in America.* New Haven, Connecticut: Yale University Press, 1984.

25. Cros Sandoval, Mercedes. *Mariel and Cuban National Identity.* Miami, Florida: Editorial SIBI, 1986.

26. Dávalos, Fernando. *La frontera en Mariel.* La Habana, Cuba: Unión de Escritores y Artistas de Cuba, 1983.

27. De Varona, Esperanza B. *Cuban Exile Periodicals at the University of Miami. An Annotated Bibliography.* SALALM, no.19. Madison, Wisconsin: University of Wisconsin Press, 1987.

28. Dominguez, Jorge I. "U.S. Immigration Policies Towards Cuba." In Western Hemisphere Immigration and United States Foreign Policy, edited by Christopher Mitchell. Pittsburgh, Pennsylvania: Pennsylvania State Press, 1992.

29. Engstrom, David W. *Decision Making Adrift: The Carter Administration and the Mariel Boatlift.* New York, New York: Rowman and Littlefield Publishers, 1997.

30. García, María Cristina. *Havana USA: Cuban Exiles and Cuban Americans in South Florida, 1959-1994.* Berkeley, California: University of California Press, 1996.

31. García Saavedra, Vivian. *El Caso de la Embajada del Perú y el Mariel: Exodo masivo de Cubanos.* Miami, Reencuentro Cubano, 1981.

32. Geldof, Lynn. *Cubans.* London: Bloomsbury Publishing Ltd., 1991.

33. Gernard, Renne. *The Cuban Americans.* Boston, Massachussets: Chelsea House, 1988.

34. Gonzáles, Diana H., and Clyde B. McCoy. *The Mariel Immigrants and Refugees.* Coral Gables: Florida: University of Miami, School of Medicine, Department of Psychiatry, 1982.

35. Grenier, Guillermo J., and Alex Stepick, eds. *Miami Now! Immigration, Ethnicity and Social Change.* Gainesville, Florida: University of Florida Press, 1992.

36. Haines, David , Editor. *Refugees in the United States: A Reference Handbook.* Westport, Connecticut: Greenwood Press, 1985.

37. Hamm, Mark S. *The Abandoned Ones: the Imprisonment and Uprising of the Mariel Boat People.* Boston, Massachussets: Northeastern University Press, 1995.

38. Haskins, James. *The New Americans: Cuban Boat People.* Hillside, New Jersey: Enslow Publishers, 1982.

39. Hernández, Rafael. *La política inmigratoria de Estados Unidos y la Revolución Cubana.* La Habana, Cuba: Centro de Estudios sobre América, 1980.

40. Hufker, Brian. *From Freedom Flotilla to America's Burden: the Social Redefinition of the Mariel Immigrants.* Tucson, Arizona: Arizona State University, 1987.

41. "Immigrants and Refugees: The Caribbean and South Florida." *Dialogue Series, no.2.* Miami, Florida: Florida International University, Latin American and Caribbean Studies Center, March 1981.

42. Jorge, Antonio. "Refugees and Immigrants: The Last Two Decades," In *Perspectives on Recent Refugee and Immigrant Waves into South Florida.* Dialogue Series, no.8. Miami, Florida: Florida International University, Latin American and Caribbean Studies Center, 1982.

43. Jorge, Antonio, and Raúl Moncarz. "Cubans in South Florida: The Political Economy of Exile And Immigration," In *Immigrant Communities in America,* edited by John Bodner. Champaign-Urbana, Illinois: University of Illinois Press, 1983.

44. Kirkpatrick, Jeanne J. *Cuba and the Cubans.* Washington, D.C.:The Cuban American Foundation, 1983.

45. Larzelere, Alex. *The 1980 Cuban Boatlift: Castro's Play—America's Dilemma.* Washington,D.C.: National Defense University Press, 1988.

46. Llanes, José. *Cuban Americans: Masters of Survival.* Cambridge, Massachussets: Abt Books, 1982.

47. Loescher, Gil, and John A. Scalan. *Calculated Kindness: Refugees and America's Half-Open Door: 1945 to the Present.* New York, New York: The Free Press, 1986.

48. Lynch, Michael J. *Race and Criminal Justice.* New York, New York: Harrow and HestonPublishers, 1991.

49. MacCorkle, Lyn. *Cubans in the United States: A Bibliography for Research in Social and Behavioral Sciences, 1960-1983.* Wesport, Connecticut: Greenwood Press, 1984.

50. Masud-Piloto, Félix Robert. *With Open Arms: Cuban Migration to the United States.* Lanham, Maryland: Rowman and Littlefield, *1988.*

51. ____. *From Welcome Exiles to Illegal Immigrants: Cuban Migration to the U.S.* Lanham, Maryland: Rowman and Littlefield, 1996.

52. Matthews, Carey. *Strike from Mariel.* Miami, Florida: First Commonwealth Press, 1983.

53. Mazarr, Michael J. *Semper Fidel: America and Cuba, 1776-1988.* Baltimore, Maryland: The Nautical and Aviation Publishing Company of America, 1988.

54. McCoy, Clyde B., Duane McBridge, J.Bryan Page, and Diana H. Gonzáles. "The Post-Revolutionary Immigration of Cubans in the United States, January 1959-January 1981," *Final Report: The Ethnography of Drug Abuse Among Cubans in Miami.* Coral Gables, Florida: University of Miami, School of Medicine, Department of Psychiatry, 1981.

55. McCoy, Clyde B., and Diana H. Gonzáles. *Cuban Immigration and Immigrants in Florida and the United States: Implication for Immigration Policy.* Monograph, no.3. Gainesville, Florida: The University of Florida, Bureau of Economic and Business Research, 1985.

56. Moncarz, Raúl. "The Cuban Migration to the United States," *Contemporary American Migration.* Boston, Massachussets: Twayne, 1982.

57. Montaner, Carlos Alberto. *Cuba, Castro, and the Caribbean.* Translated by Nelson Duran. New Brunswick, New Jersey: Transaction Books, 1985.

58. Olson, James S. and Judith E. Olson. *Cuban Americans: From Trauma to Triumph.* New York: Twayne Publishers, 1995.

59. Pedraza-Bailey,Silvia. *Political and Economic Immigrants in America: Cubans and Mexicans.* Austin, Texas: University of Texas Press, 1985.

60. Pérez-Vidal, Angel. *Muchas Gracias-Marielitos!: una historia verdadera y siete cuentos imaginados.* Miami, Florida: Ediciones Universal, 1988.

61. Philipson, Lorrin, and Rafael Llerena. *Freedom Flights: Cuban Refugees Talk About Life Under Castro and How They Fled His Regime.* New York, New York: Random House,

1980.

62. Portes, Alejandro. *Adaptation Process of Cuban (Mariel) and Haitian Refugees in South Florida, 1983-1987.* Ann Arbor, Michigan: Inter-University Consortium for Political and Social Research, 1992.

63. Portes, Alejandro. *Three Years later: The Adaptation Process of 1980 (Mariel) Cuban and Haitian Refugees in South Florida.* Miami: Florida International University, 1985.

64. Portes, Alejandro, and Robert L. Bach. *Latin Journey: Cuban and Mexican Immigrants in the United States.* Berkeley, California: University of California Press, 1985.

65. Portes, Alejandro, and Alex Stepick. *City on the Edge: The Transformation of Miami.* Berkeley and Los Angeles: University of California Press, 1993.

66. Rieff, David. *The Exile: Cuba in the Heart of Miami.* New York: Simon & Schuster, 1993.

67. Rivera, Mario Antonio. *Decision and Structure: U.S.Refugee Policy in the Mariel Crisis.* Lanham, Maryland: University Press of America, 1991.

68. Rivero, A. *Mariel Refugees in the Dade County Public School System: Report on Attitudinal Research Survey.* Miami, Florida: Dade County Public School System, 1981.

69. Robbins, Carla Anne. *The Cuban Threat.* New York, New York: McGraw-Hill Book Co., 1983.

70. Rodríguez, Rodolfo, and Bienvenido Madan. *Golden Ages of the Cuban Exiles, 1959-1983.* New York, New York: 1983.

71. Rosas, Eugenio. *De Cayo Hueso a Mariel.* Puerto Rico: Ramallo Bros, 1982.

72. Scheina, Robert L. *The Cuban Exodus of 1980.* U.S. Naval Institute Proceedings, 1980

73. Shalloup, Troy. *The Social Construction of the Mariel Prison Riots.* Tucson, Arizona: Arizona State University Press, 1991.

74. Smith, Wayne S. *The Closets of Enemies: A Personal and Diplomatic Account of U.S-Cuban Relations Since 1957.* New York, New York: W.W. Norton, 1987.

75. Stepick, Alex and Guillermo Grenier. "Cubans in Miami" In *In the Barrios: Latinos and the Underclass Debate*,edited by Joan Moore and Raquel Pinder Hughes, 79-100. New

York: Russell Sage Foundation, 1993.

76. Szapocznik, José, Raquel E.Cohen, and Roberto E. Hernández, eds. *Coping with Adolescent Refugees: the Mariel Boatlift.* New York, New York: Praeger, 1985

77. Teitlebaum, Michael S. *Latin American Migration: The Problem for U.S. Foreign Policy.* New York, New York: Council on Foreign Relations, 1985.

78. Thomas, Hugh S., Georges A Faurioul, and Juan Carlos Weiss. *The Cuban Revolution 25 Years Later.* Boulder, Colorado: Westview Press, 1984.

79. Thomas, John F. "Cuban Refugee Program." In *Cuban Refugee Programs,* edited by Carlos E. Cortes. New York, New York: Arno Press, 1980.

80. Torres, María de los Angeles. "From Exiles to Minorities: The Politics of Cuban Americans," In *Latinos and the Political System,* edited by F. Chris García. Notre Dame, Indiana: University of Notre Dame Press, 1988.

81. Villaverde, Fernando. *Crónicas del Mariel.* Miami, Florida: Ediciones Universal, 1992.

82. Wallack, John P. "Fidel Castro and the United States Press." In *The Selling of Fidel Castro,* Edited by William E. Ratcliff. New Brunswick, New Jersey: Transaction Books, 1987.

83. Weiss-Fagen, Patricia. *Immigration, Emigration and Asylum Policies on Cuba.* Washington,D.C.: Refugee Policy Group, 1984.

84. Willbanks, Williams. *Murder in Miami: An Analysis of Homicide Patterns and Trends in Dade County (Miami) Florida, 1917-1983.* Lanham, Maryland: University Press of America, 1984.

85. Zelinsky, Wilbur. *The Cultural Geography of the United States.* Inglewood Cliffs, N.J.: Prentice Hall, 1992.

86. Zucker, Naomi Flink, and Norman L. Zucker. *The Guarded Gate: The Reality of the American Refugee Policy.* San Diego, California: Harcourt, Brace Jovanovich, 1987.

87. ———. "A Foreign Policy Compass: Refugees and Assylum Seekers" In *Desperate Crossings: Seeking Refugees in America.* Armonk New York: ME Sharpe, 1996.

Academic Journals and Books Reviews

88. Aguilar, Luis E. "Castro's Failed Revolution," *Problems of Communism* , (July-August 1983): 46-50.

89. Aguirre, Benigno E. "Differential Migration of Cuban Social Races." *Latin American Research Review*, 11, No. 1 (1976): 103-24.

90. _____. "Cuban Mass Migration and the Social Construction of Deviants," *Bulletin of Latin American Research*, 13 (1994): 155-183.

91. _____. "Aid for Cuban Artists," *Nuestro*, (January-February 1982): 11.

92. Aguirre, Benigno E. , Rogelio Sáenz, and Brian Sinclair James. "Marielitos Ten Years Later: The Scarface Legacy," *Social Science Quaterly*, (1998).

93. Alba, Richard and Victor Nee. "Rethinking Assimilation Theory for a New Era of Immigration," *International Migration Review*, 31(1997): 826-874.

94. Argüelles, Lourdes. "Un año después del Mariel," *Areito*, No.7 (1981): 57-59.

95. Azicri, Max. "Politics of Exile: Trends and Dynamics of Political Change Among Cuban-Americans," *Cuban Studies/Estudios Cubanos*, 11/12 (July 1981- January 1982): 55-74.

96. Bach, Robert L. "Cuba in Crisis," *Migration Today*, 8 (1980) :15-18.

97. _____. "The New Cuban Exodus: Political and Economic Motivations." *Caribbean Review*, 11, No.1 (1982): 22- 25, 58-60.

98. _____. "The New Cuban Immigrants :Their Backgrounds and Prospects," *Monthly Labor Review*, 103 (October (1980): 39-46.

99. _____. "Socialist Construction and Cuban Emigration: Explorations into Mariel." *Cuban Studies/ Estudios Cubanos*, 15 (Summer 1985): 19-36.

100. Bach, Robert L., Jennifer B. Bach, and Timothy Triplett. "The Flotilla 'Entrants': Latest and Most Controversial," *Cuban Studies/ Estudios Cubanos*, 11/12 (July 1981/ January 1982): 29-48.

101. Baloyra, Enrique A. "Making Waves: A View of the

Cuban Community in the U.S.," *Cuban Studies/ Estudios Cubanos,* 11/12 (July 1981//January 1982): 75-80.

102. Barquet, Jesús J. "Keys To Understand The Cubans in Exile: The Mariel Generation," *Revue Francais d"Etudes Americaines,* No.41, (1989): 345-356.

103. Batsalel, Kenneth Aaron. "The Limit(s) of Commitment: Journal Reflections on the Mariel Cuban Repatriation Panel Review Hearings." *Dialectical Anthropology,* 17, No.1, (1992): 85-111.

104. Blue, Philip Y. "Law and Crime—The Abandoned Ones: The Imprisonment and Uprising of the Mariel Boat People by Mark S. Hamm," *Library Journal,* 12, No.9, (May 15, 1995): 82.

105. Borjas, George J. "The Earnings of the Male Hispanic Immigrants in the United States," *Industrial and Labor Relations Review,* 35 (April 1982): 343-353.

106. Borneman, John. "Emigres as Bullets/Immigration as Penetrations of the Marielitos," *Journal of Popular Culture* 20, 3 (1986): 73-92.

107. Boswell, Thomas D. "The Cuban- American Homeland in Miami," *Journal of Cultural Geography* 13, 2 (1993): 133-148.

108. Boswell, Thomas D. and Manuel Rivero. "Cubans in America: A Minority Group Comes of Age," *Focus, American Geographical Society,* 35 (April 1985):2-9.

109. Boswell, Thomas D., Guarioné M. Díaz, and Lisandro Pérez. "Socioeconomic Context of Cuban Americans." *Journal of Cultural Geography,* (Fall/Winter 1982) :29-41.

110. Card, David. "The Impact of the Mariel Boatlift on the Miami Labor Market," *Industrial & Labor Relations Review,* 43, No.2, (Jan 1990): 245-257.

111. Carroll, Mary. "The Abandoned Ones: The Imprisonment and Uprising of the Mariel Boat People by Mark S. Hamm," *Booklist,* 91, No.19-20, (June 1, 1995).

112. Castillo, Siro del. "A Plea to De-stigmatize Mariel." Translated by Judith C. Faerron, *Caribbean Review",* (Fall 1984): 7.

113. Cavender, Gray, and Brian Hufker. "From Freedom Flotilla to America's Burden," *The Sociological Quarterly,* 31 (1990): 321-335.

114. Chisholm, Shirley. "U.S. Policy and Black Refugees," *A. Q. J. of Opinion*, 12 (1-2) (1982): 22-24.

115. Cohon, Donald J., Jr. "Psychological Adaptation and Dysfunction Among Refugees," *International Migration Review*, 15 (Spring/Summer 1981): 255-275.

116. Copeland, Ronald. "The 1980 Cuban Crisis: Some Observations," *Journal of Refugee Resettlement*, 1 (August 1981):22-33.

117. _____. "The Cuban Boatlift of 1980: Strategies in Federal Crisis Management," *Annals of the American Academy of Political Science*, (May 1983): 138-150.

118. "Cuban/Haitian Entrant Act of 1980," *Migration Today*, 8 (1980): 26.

119. DeFoor, J Allison, II. "Mariel Boatlift: a Failed Mission," *Update* (Historical Association of Southern Florida), 12 (3) (1985): 11-13.

120. De la Campa, Román. "The Latino Diáspora in the United States: Sojourns from a Cuban Past," *Public Culture*, (Winter 1994): 293-317.

121. Demmi, L., and K. Doxsey. "Encountering the Recent Influx of Cuban Refugees in the Emergency Department," *Journal of Emergency Nursing*, 7 (1981): 11-13.

122. Díaz-Briquets, Sergio. "Demographic and Related Determinants of Recent Cuban Emigration," *International Migration Review*, 17 (Spring 1983): 95-119.

123. Diaz-Briquets, Sergio, and Lisandro Pérez. "Cuba: The Demography of Revolution," *Population Bulletin*, No.36, (April 1981).

124. _____. "Fertility Decline in Cuba: A Socioeconomic Interpretation," *Population and Development Review*, 8 (September 1982): 513-37.

125. Dixon, Heriberto. "A Look at the Socio-Economic Adaptation of the Mariel Cubans," *Literary Journal*, 4 July 1983): 4-7.

126. _____. "Who Ever Heard of a Black Cuban?" *Afro-Hispanic Review*, 1 (September 1982): 10-12.

127. _____. "The Cuban-American Counterpoint: Black Cubans in the United States," *Dialectical Anthropology*, 13 (1988): 227-239.

128. Doherty, Carroll J. "Influx of Cubans Forces Clinton to

Halt Automatic Asylum: Moving to Prevent a Replay of 1980 Mariel Boatlift, President Orders Refugees Taken to Guantanamo," *Congressional Quarterly Weekly Report*, 52 (August 20, 1994): 2464-2465.

129. Domínguez, Jorge I. "Cuba in the 1980s," *Problems of Communism*, (March/April 1981): 48-59.

130. Duany, Jorge. "Hispanics in the United States: Cultural Diversity and Identity," *Caribbean Studies*, 22 (1989): 1- 25.

131. Eaton, William W, and Roberta Garrison. "Mental Health in Mariel Cubans and Haitian Boat People," *International Migration Review*, 26, No.4, (Winter 1992): 1395-1415.

132. Estevez, Guillermo A. "Resettling the Cuban Refugees in New Jersey," *Migration Today*, 11 (1983): 27- 33.

133. _____. "Ethics, Scholarship and the Justice Professional: The Tragic Case of the Mariel Cubans," *The Justice Professional*, 6 (1992): 135-154.

134. Etzioni, Armitai. "Refugee Resettlement: The Infighting in Washington," *The Public Interest*, 29 (Fall 1981): 15-29.

135. Fernández, Gastón A. "The Flotilla Entrants: Are They Different?" *Cuban Studies/Estudios Cubanos*, 12 (January 1982): 49-54.

136. _____. "The Freedom Flotilla: A Legitimacy Crisis of Cuban Socialism?," *Journal of Inter-American Studies and World Affairs*, 24 (May 1982): 183-210.

137. _____. "Conflicting Interpretations of the Freedom Flotilla Entrants, the Mariel Flotilla Again," *Cuban Studies / Estudios Cubanos*, 14 (1) (1984): 49-51.

138. Fernández, Gastón A., and León Narváez. "Refugees and Human Rights in Costa Rica: the Mariel Cubans," *International Migration Review*, 21: 406-416.

139. Fernández, Gastón A., and León Narváez. "Bibliography of Cuban Immigration / Adaptation to the United States," *Cuban Studies / Estudios Cubanos*, 15 (Summer 1985): 61-72.

140. Fernández-Kelly, M. et. al. "Divided Fates: Immigrant Children in a Restructured U.S. Economy," *International Immigration Review* 28, 4 (1994): 662-89.

141. Fox, Geoffrey. "The Cuban Exodus and the U.S. Press," *Cuban Update*, 3 (September 1980) : 4-6.

142. Fradd, Sandra. "Cubans to Cuban Americans: As-

similation in the United States." *Migration Today*, 11 (4-5) (1983): 34-42.

143. Frankenhoff, Charles A. "Cuban, Haitian Refugees in Miami: Public Policy Needs for Growth From Welfare To Mainstream," *Migration Today*, 3 (1985): 6-13.

144. García, Margarite. "The Last Days in Cuba: Personal Accounts of the Circumstances of the Exit," *Migration Today*, 11 (1983): 13-22.

145. Gardinen, E. "Cuban/Haitian Unaccompanied Minors," *Child Welfare*, 60 (1981): 359-362.

146. Garza, Mariel. "Justice for Sale: Faster Justice for Those Who Can Pay," *Cal-J*, 22 (1991): 481-2.

147. Gastón, C.E. "La Verand Solie les Exiliados del Mariel," *Cuban Collection*, (June 3, 1983).

148. Geltmen, Emanuel. "The Cuban Exodus—A Taste of Freedom," *Dissent*, (Summer 1980): 263-264.

149. Gil, Rosa María. "Issues in the Delivery of Mental Health Services to Cuban Entrants," *Migration Today*, 11 (1983) : 43-48.

150. González, Diana H. "More on Cuban Immigration," *Humanist Sociology*, 5 (1980): 1-4.

151. Gonzáles, Diana H. and John Bryan Page. "Cuban Women, Sex Role Conflicts and the Use of Prescription Drugs," *Journal of Psychoactive Drugs*, 13 (January-March 1981): 47-51.

152. Gordon, A.M. "Caribbean Basin Refugees: the Impact of Cubans and Haitians on Health in South Florida," *The Journal of the Florida Medical Association*, 69: 532-527.

153. ____. "Nutritional Status of Cuban Refugees: Field Study on the Health and Nature of Refugees Processed at Opa Locka, Florida," *The American Journal of Clinical Nutrition*, 35 (1982): 582-590.

154. Greenbaum, Susan D. "Afro-Cubans in Exile: Tampa, Florida, 1886-1984," *Cuban Studies/ Estudios Cubanos*, 15 (1985): 59-72.

155. Harmon R.B, R. Rosner, and M. Wiederlight. "The Mariel Refugee and the New York Criminal Court," *New York City Dept. Of Mental Health,*:32, No.3 (1987): 725-735.

156. Hawk, Kate Dupes. "Politics, Poison and Plague: Mariel Boat Lift Legacy," *The Journal of the Florida Medical As-*

sociation, 8, No.9, (September 1993): 619.

157. Hihl, Donald G. "The Cuban-Haitian Entrant 'Program'-A Critique," *Migration Today*, 8 (1980): 27.

158. Hoffman, Fred. "Mariel Cuban Refugees in the American Psychiatric Care System," *Sociological Practice Review*, V1, No.2, (Aug 1, 1990).

159. Hufker, Brian; and Gary Cavender. "From Freedom Flotilla to America's Burden: the Social Construction of the Mariel Immigrants," *Sociological Quarterly*, 31 (2) (1990): 321-335.

160. Huyck, Earl E.; Rona Fields. "Impact of Resettlement on Refugee Children," *International Migration Review*, 15 (Spring/Summer 1981): 246-54.

161. "L'Immigration: les Annees 1980," *Revue Francais d' Etudes Americaines*, 14 (July 1989): 259-61.

162. Jasso, Guillermina. "Book Review—Decision and Structure: U.S. Refugee Policy in the Mariel Crisis, by Mario Antonio Rivera," *Journal of Policy Analysis & Management*, 12, No.2, (Spring 1993): 403-406.

163. Jensen, Leif; and Alejandro Portes. "The Enclave and Entrants: Patterns of Ethnic Enterprise in Miami Before and After Mariel," *American Sociological Review*, 57, No.3 (June 1992): 411-420.

164. _____. Cubans in South Florida: A Social Science Approach," *Metas*, 1 (Fall 1980): 37-87.

165. Kennedy, Edward M. "Refugee Act of 1980," *International Migration Review*, 15 (Spring/Summer 1981): 141-156.

166. Kirschten, Dick. "Anatomy of a Flip-Flop," *National Journal*, 25, No.5, (Jan 30, 1993): 313.

167. Lega, Leonore I. "The 1980 Cuban Refugees: Some of Their Initial Attitudes Toward Their Future in a New Society," *Migration Today*, 11 (1983): 23-26.

168. LeoGrande, William M. "Cuban Policy Recycled," *Foreign Policy*, (Spring 1982): 105-119.

169. Loescher, Gilburt and John Scalan. "U.S. Foreign Policy, 1959-80: Impact on Refugee Flows From Cuba," *Annals of the American Academy of Political and Social Science*, 467 (May 1983): 116.

170. Macchi, Mariel E. "El convenio de la Unión de París,"

Realidad Económica, No.1, (1988): 97-109.

171. Massey, Douglas., and Kathleen M. Sohnabel. "Recent Trends in Hispanic Immigration to the United States," *International Migration Review*, 17 (Summer 1983): 212-244.

172. Massey, Douglas, and Brendan P. Mullin, "Processes of Hispanic and Black Spatial Assimilation.," *The American Journal of Sociology*, 89 (1984): 836-71.

173. McCoy, Clyde B., J. Bryan Page, and Diana H. Gonzáles. "Cuban and Other Latin Immigration to Florida," *Florida Outlook*, 16 (June 1982): 77-80.

174. McHugh, Kevin, Inés Miyares, and Emily Skop. "The Magnetism of Miami: Segmented Paths in Cuban Migration," *The Geographical Review*, 87,4 (1998):504-519.

175. Mohl, Raymond. "An Ethnic 'Boiling Pot': Cubans and Haitians in Miami," *Journal of Ethnic Studies*, 13 (Summer 1985): 51-74.

176. _____. "The Politics of Ethnicity in Miami," *Migration World*, 14 (1986): 7-11.

177. _____. "Race, Ethnicity, and Urban Politics in the Miami Metropolitan Area," *Florida Environmental and Urban Issues*, (April 1982): 2-6, 23-25.

178. Montaner, Carlos Alberto. "The Roots of Anti-Americanism in Cuba," *Caribbean Review*, 13, (Spring 1984): 13- 16, 42-46.

179. Moncarz, Raúl. "Immigrant Economic Adjustment and Family Organization: The Cuban Success Story Reexamined', *International Migration Review*, 20 (Spring 1986): 4-10.

180. Palmieri, Victor H. "Cuban-Haitian Fact Sheet," *Migration Today*, 8 (1980): 9.

181. _____. "The Refugees: What 'Infighting'?, The Refugees Controversy," *Public Interest*, 68, (1982): 88-92.

182. Pedraza- Bailey, Silvia. "Cubans and Mexicans in the United States: The Function of Political and Economic Migration," *Cuban Studies/Estudios Cubanos*, 11-12, (July 1981/January 1982): 79-97.

183. _____. "Cuba's Exiles: Portrait of a Refugee Migration," *International Migration Review*, 19 (1), (1985): 4-34.

184. Pérez, Brittmarie Janson. "Fringes of the Exodus: Revitalization Through Emigration," *Contribution to Anthrop-*

ology, 2 (Spring 1983): 40-45.

185. Pérez, Lisandro. "Cubans and Mexicans in the United States," *Cuban Studies/Estudios Cubanos*, 11/12, (July 1981/January 1982): 99-103.

186. ____. "Cubans in the United States," *Annals of the Academy of Political and Social Science*, 487, (September 1986):126.

187. ____. "Immigrant Economic Adjustment and Family Organization: The Cuban Success Story Reexamined," *International Migration Review*, 20, (Spring 1986):4-10.

188. Pérez, R. "Provisions of Mental Health Series During a Disaster: the Cuban Immigration of 1980," *Journal of Community Psychology*, 10: 40-47.

189. Petersen, Mark P. "The Flotilla Entrants: Social Psychological Perspective on Their Employment," *Cuban Studies/Estudios Cubanos*, 12, (July 1982): 81-85.

190. ____. "Work Attitudes of Mariel Boatlift Refugees," *Cuban Studies/ Estudios Cubanos* 14 (2) (1984): 1- 19.

191. Portes, Alejandro. "The Social Origins of the Cuban Enclave Economy of Miami," *Sociological Perspectives*, 30 (October 1987): 340-371.

192. Portes, Alejandro, Juan M. Clark, and Robert D. Manning. "After Mariel: a Survey of the Resettlement Experiences of 1980 Cuban Refugees in Miami," *Cuban Studies/Estudios Cubanos*, 15, (Summer 1985): 37-59.

193. Portes, Alejandro and Ming Zhou. "The New Second Generation: Segmented Assimilation and Its Variants," *The Annals of the Academy of Political and Social Science*. 530, (1993): 74-96.

194. Portes, Alejandro, et. al. "Assimilation or Consciousness: Perceptions of U.S. Society Among Recent Latin American Immigrants to the U.S.," *Social Forces*, 59, (September 1980): 200-224.

195. Portes, Alejandro and Rafael Mozo. "The Political Adaptation Process of Cubans and Other Ethnic Minorities in the United States: A Preliminary Analysis," *International Migration Review*, 19, (Spring 1985): 35-63.

196. Portes Alejandro., and L. Jensen. "The Enclave and the Entrants-Patterns of Ethnic Enterprise in Miami Before and After Mariel," *American Sociological Review*, 54, No.6,

(1989): 929-949.

197. Portes, Alejandro, David Kyle, and William W. Eaton. "Mental Illness and Help-Seeking Behavior Among Mariel Cuban and Haitian Refugees in South Florida," *Journal of Health & Social Behavior,* 33 (4), (December 1992): 283-298.

198. Portes, Alejandro, and Alex Stepick "Unwelcome Immigrants: the Labor Market Experiences of 1980 (Mariel) Cuban and Haitian Refugees in South Florida," *American Sociological Review,* 50, (August 1985): 493-514.

199. Portes, Alejandro., Alex Stepick, and C. Truelove. "The Adaptation Process of 1980 (Mariel) Cuban and Haitian Refugees in South Florida—3 years later," *Population Research and Policy Review,* 5, No.1, (1986): 83-94.

200. "Revillard, -Mariel: Les Conventions Internationals Relatives aux Associations." *J. Droit-International* 119 (Ap/Je 1992):299-318.

201. Rich, B. Ruby:, and Lourdes.Argüelles. "Homosexuality, Homophobia, And Revolution: Notes Towards An Understanding Of The Cuban And Gay Male Experience, Part II." *Signs* 11 (1) (1985): 120-136.

202. ____. Refugee Chess: Policy by Default. *Caribbean Review* 13 (4) (1984): 4-6, 36-39.

203. Roca, Octavio "An Exile's Home Away from Home." *Insight,* 4, No.41 (Oct 10, 1988): 60-61.

204. Rodríguez Chavez, Ernesto, "Tendencias actuales del flujo migratorio cubano." *Caribbean Studies* 26 1/2) (1993): 127-159.

205. Rogg, Eleanor Meyer: "Incorporation of Cuban Exiles," *Cuban Studies/ Estudios Cubanos,* 11/12 (July 1981/January 1982): 25-28.

206. Rogg, Eleanor Meyer and Joan J. Homberg, "The Assimilation: Cubans in the United States," *Migration Today,* 11 (1983): 8.

207. Rothchild, John. "The Cuban Connection and Gringo Press." *Columbian Journal Review,* 23 (September/October 1984): 48-51.

208. Rumbaut, Ruben. "The Crucible Within: Ethnic Identity, Self-Esteem, and Segmented Assimilation Among Children of Immigrants." *International Migration Review,* 28, 4 (1994): 748-94.

209. Simon, Rita J. "Old Minorities, New Immigrants: Aspirations, Hopes, and Fears." *The Annals of Political and Social Science*, 530 (1993): 61-73.

210. Scalan John and Gilburt Loescher "U.S. Foreign Policy, 1959-80: Impact on Refugee Flow from Cuba." *Annals of the American Academy of Political and Social Science*, 467 (May 1983) : 116-137.

211. _____. "Mass Asylum and Human Rights in American Foreign Policy." *Pre-publication draft for publication in the Political Science Quarterly* (March 1982).

212. "Scholars Call for Negotiation,." *Black Issues Higher Education*, 11, No.14 (September 8 1994): 16.

213. Smither, Robert. "American Ambivalence Toward Refugees." *Migration Today*, 8 (1980): 20-24.

214. Stowers, Genie N .L "Political Participation , Ethnicity, and Class Status: The Case of Cubans in Miami," *Ethnic Groups*, 8 (1990): 73-90.

215. Von Blumenthal, N. "Cubans in Pachacamac, Perú." *Refugees*, (June 18, 1985): 13.

216. Weiner, M. "On International Migration and International Relations," *Population and Development Review*, 11 (3) (1985): 441-456.

217. Wilson, Kenneth L,.and Martin W. Allen, "Ethnic Enclaves: A Comparison of the Cuban and Black Economies In Miami," *American Journal of Sociology*, 86 (September 1980): 295-319.

218. Wilson, Kenneth L, .and Alejandro Portes, "Immigration Enclaves- An Analyses of the Labor-Market Experience of Cuban in Miami," *American Journal of Sociology*, 86 (September 1980): 295-319.

219. "Wisconsin Serves Cubans on Shoestring Budget," *Liberty Journal*, 105 (October 1980) :21-57.

220. Zhou, Ming. "Segmented Assimilation: Issues, Controversies, and Recent Research on the Second Generation" In *International Migration Review*, 31, 4 (1997): 957-1008.

221. Zucker, Norman L. "Contemporary American Immigration and Refugee Policy: An Overview," *Journal of Children in Contemporary Society*, 15 (Spring 1983): 5-15.

Law Journal and Other Legal Materials

222. Boswell, Richard A." Rethinking Exclusion— the Rights of Cuban Refugees Facing Indefinite Detention in the United States," 17 *Van. J. TRANSNAT'L.*925 (1984).

223. Brill, Kenneth. "The Endless Debate: Refugee Law and Policy and the 1980 Refugee Act. 32 , *"Clev.St.Law.Rev.* 117 (1983).

224. Dominguez, Eddie. "Judge Bars U.S. Repatriating Cubans," *Chicago Daily Law Bulletin,* 140, 209 (October 25, 1994).

225. Erickson, Philip. "The Saga of Indefinitely Detained Mariel Cubans," *LOY.L.A. INT'L & COMP. L.J.* 10, (Winter 1988).

226. Hahn, Richard. "Constitutional Limits on the Power to Exclude Aliens," *COLM.L.REV.,* 82, (June 1982).

227. Henkins, Louis. "The President and International Law, Agora: May the President violate Customary Law?" (pts. 1,2 &3), 80(4) AM. J. INT'L L. 913 (1986), 80 (4) AM.J. INT'L. 930 (1986), 81 (2) AM. J. INT'L. 371 (1986).

228. Hopson, Susan B. "Immigration— Indefinite Detention of Excluded Aliens, Held Illegal," 17 *EX. INT'L L.J.* 101 (1982).

229. Analysis of García-Mir v. Smith, *TRAS 10 SUFFOLK NAT'L L.REV.* 279 (1986).

230. Jones, Thomas David. "A Human Rights Tragedy: the Cuban and Haitian Refugee Crisis Revisited," *9 GEO. IMMIGR. L.J.* 479 (1995).

231. Kemple, M.D. "Legal Fictions Mask Human Suffering— the Detention of the Mariel Cubans Constitutional, Statutory, International-Law, and Human Considerations," *62 S. CAL. L. REV.* 1733 (1989).

232. Kleinberg, Howard. "Blacks Need Not Apply: Immorality of Immigration Policy Based in Miami," *L.A. Daily J.,* July 29, 1991, at 6.T.

233. Kuntz, Katherine. "Making theUnited States Accountable Under Customary International Law," *10 DENV. J. INT'L. & POLY* 369 (1981).

234. Kuzban, Ira. "A Critical Analysis of Refugee Law," *36 U. Miami L. Rev. 865* (1986).

235. "Manual for Representing Cubans in Gaining Release and Immigration Status," LAW'S COMM. HUM. RTS. (New York, N.Y.) 1989.

236. Leich, Marian Nash. "Contemporary Practice of the United States Relating to International Law," *70 AM. J. INT'L L.* 1044 (1985).

237. Leshaw, Gary. "Atlanta's Cuban Detainees: A Retrospective Check," *ATLANTA LAWYER*. 4th. Quarter, 6-28.

238. Litwin, Paul J. "Alien's -Detention- Indefinite Detention of Illegal Aliens No Longer Indefinite," 6 *SUFFOLK TRANSNAT'L. L.J.* 333 (1982).

239. Lyons, David. "Asylum Rule Change Decried: Administration Says it has Discretion to Alter 1966 Cuban Adjustment Act," *NAT'L L.J.*, Sept. 5, 1994 at A6.

240. Mailman, Stanley. "The Cuban-Haitian Bill and its Sleepers," *N.Y. L.J.*, Nov. 5, 1980 at 1.

241. _____. "First Board Ruling in Refugee Case," *N.Y. L.J.*, Nov. 5, 1980 at 1.

242. Martin, David A. "The Refugee Act of 1980: It's Past and Future," TRANSACT'L L. PROBLEMS REFUGEES 1982 *MICH. YEARBOOK INT'L L. STUD.* 91, (D.M. Levy ed., 1982).

243. Miller, L. Robert. "How the Grinch Stole Christmas— and Then Had to Give it Back," The *Los Angeles Daily Journal,* 93 (November 25, 1980): 3.

244. "The Freedom Flotilla Six Years Later; from Mariel to Minnesota," *MINN LAW'S INT'L HUM. RTS COMM.* (Minneapolis, Minn.) 1986.

245. Montgomery, L. Paul. "38 Cuban Women Linger in Cells Awaiting Status Ruling: Guilty Until Proven Innocent," *L.A. DAILY J.*, Nov. 25, 1980 at 3.

246. Moya, Frank. "Court Frees Cuban Refugee After Deportation Stipends," *NAT'L.. L.J.*, July 27, 1981 at 4.

247. Reiss, Sandra B. "The International Covenant on Civil and Political Rights: Can it Free the Cuban Detainees," 6 *EMORY INT'L. REV.* 577 (1992).

248. Rice, Marc. "More Uncertainly for Refugees After Appeals Court Ruling," 140 *CHI. DAILY L. BULL.* Dec. 21, 1944 at N249.

249. Rosenbaum, B. David. "The Constitutional Rights of Excluded Aliens: Proposed Limitations on the Indefinite

Detention of the Cuban Refugees," 70 *GEO. L.J.* 1303 (1982).
250. Rosewicz, Barbara. "Justice Department to Offer Proposal to Resolve Refugee Dispute," *L.A. Daily J.*, Jan.14, 1981 at 5.

Public Documents

251. (Congressional documents, hearings, bulletins, government, publications, etc.

252. Atwood, J. Bryan. "The Cuban Exodus." *Foreign Affairs Memorandum. U.S. Department of State,* (May 1980): 1-6.

253. Boswell, Thomas D., Guarioné M. Díaz, and Manuel Rivero. The Demographic Characteristics of the Pre-Mariel Cubans Living in the State of Florida:1980. Washington D.C.: Community Relations Service, *U.S. Department of Justice,* 1984.

254. Bowen, Robert L., ed. A Report of the Cuban-Haitian Task Force, Cuban-Haitian Task Force, *Department of State,* Washington, D.C., November 1, 1980, 116p.

255. Buchanan, Susan. Cuban-Haitian Entrant Social Service Program, Community Relations Service, *Department of Justice,* New York, Date Unavailable.

256. Burns, Edward K. The Cuban Boatlift. INS Reporter, *US. Department of Justice,* Immigration and Naturalization Service. Winter 1981-82: pp.4-7.

257. Carosso, John. Cuban/Haitian Entrant Program Operational Manual. Cuban-Haitian Task Force, *Department of Health and Human Services,* Washington, D.C., March 20, 1981, 42p.

258. Clark, David D. The Mariel Cuban Problem, *State of New York, Dept. of Correctional Services,* Division of Program Planning, Research and Evaluation, Albany, NY, 1991.

259. ____. The Mariel Cuban Reimbursement Program: Final Report, *State of New York, Dept. of Correctional Services,* Albany, NY, 1994.

260. Cobb, David. "FEMA and the Freedom Flotilla," *Emergency Management Magazine,* 1: (Fall1980): 4331-37A.

261. *Commission on Immigration and Refugee Policy.* U.S.

Immigration Policy and National Interest. Washington, D.C.: U.S. Government Printing Office, 1981.

262. U.S. Congress. Committee on the Judiciary. Caribbean Refugee Crisis: Cubans and Haitians, Hearing Before the *Committee on the Judiciary, U.S. Senate.* Washington, D.C.: U.S. Government Printing Office, 1980.

263. Copeland, Ronald. "Cuban and Haitian Migration," *Department of State Bulletin.* (October 1981) : 78-79.

264. _____. "Cuban-Haitian Refugees," *Department of State Bulletin,* (August 1980): 79-82.

265. _____. "Cuban Refugees," *Department of State Bulletin,* (June 1980): 68-71.

266. *Dade County Planning Department, Research Division,* Social and Economic Problems Among Cuba and Haitian Entrant Groups in Dade County Florida: Trends and Indications," Miami, Florida, 1981.

267. Davis, J. The Missing Link to Credibility Data. *Report to Miami Citizens Against Crime Committee,* Miami, Florida, 1982.

268. Eig, Larry M. Indefinite Detention of Freedom Flotilla Cubans: A History of the Judicial Response, Washington, D.C., *Library of Congress, Congressional Research Service,* 1986.

269. Enders, Thomas O. "Cuban and Haitian Migration," *Department of State Bulletin,* (October 1981): 78-79.

270. "Exodus from Cuba," *Department of State Bulletin,* (July 1980): 80-1.

271. The Florida Refugee Program, Tallahassee, Fla.: Office of the Secretary, *Refugee Programs Administration,* HRS, 1991, 136 pp.

272. "Human Rights and the Refugee Crisis," *Department of State Bulletin,* (September 1982):43-45.

273. *Governor's Office of Planning and Budgeting.* The Fiscal Impact of Refugees and Entrants on State and Local Government in Florida from 1980 to the Present, Tallahassee, FL: Author, 1982.

274. Graham, R. Testimony: Final Report of the *Select Commission on Immigration and Refugee Policy,* Washington, D.C.: U.S. Government Printing Office, 1981.

275. Guide to Immigration Benefits. *INS Outreach Program,*

Immigration and Naturalization Service, Washington, D.C., 1982, 241 pp.

276. Haines, David W. Refugee Resettlement in the United States: An Annotated Bibliography on the Adjustment of Cuban, Soviet and Southeast Asian Refugees, Washington, D.C.: *Office of Refugee Resettlement, Department of Health and Human Services*, 1981, 104 pp.

277. Kessler, M.M. Operation Red, White, and Blue, May 1, 1980 - September 26, 1980, Eglin Air Force Base. *U.S Air Force Armament Division*, Office of History (Florida), December 31, 1980.

278. Leshaw, Gory. "Statement Before *U.S. House Judiciary Committee*," Subcommittee on Courts, Civil Liberties, and the Administration of Justice,(February 4, 1988).

279. Lieberman, L. The Impact of Cuban and Haitian Refugees on State Services: *Focus on Health Services Problems in Cross-Cultural Contexts* (Report No. 81-66, 81-67). Report Star Grant Project (DRST), September 1982.

280. The Mariel Injustice: in the Bicentennial of the United States Constitution. Coral Gables, Fla.: *The Commission*, 1987, 204 pp.

281. Nacci, Peter L. "The Oakdale-Atlanta Prison Disturbances: The Events, the Results," *Federal Probation*, (December 1988):3-12.

282. Pew, F.W. The Role of Forcscom in the Reception and Care of Refugees From Cuba in the Continental United States. *U.S. Army Forces Command, Office of the Chief of Staff*, Military History Office, November 1984.

283. "Refugee Admissions and Resettlement Plans for Fiscal Year 1981," *Department of State Bulletin*, No.80 (December 1980): 44-46.

284. Refugee Materials Center Bibliography. *Kansas City, Missouri: Department of Education*, Regional Office 7, May 15, 1982.

285. *U.S. Senate*. "Report to the Senate Appropriations Committee on the Cuban/Haitian Entrant Program." The Office of Refugee Resettlement, *Department of Health and Human Services* (January 13, 1982): 18 pp.

286. Rivera, Mario A., The Cuban and Haitian Influxes of 1980 and the American Response: Retrospect and Prospect,

Agency Report. U.S. *Department of State*, Cuban/Haitian Task Force.Washington, D.C., 1980.

287. Rivero, A. Mariel Refugees in the Dade County Public School System: Report on an Attitudinal Research Survey. Miami, FL: *Dade County Public School System*, 1981.

288. Silva, Helga. The Children Mariel From Shock to Integration: Cuban Refugee Children in South Florida Schools. *U.S. Department of Education*,1985.

289. Silver, Larry B., Et al. "The Cuban Immigration of 1980," *Public Health Reports*, (January-February, 1981): 100:40-8.

290. *United Nations*. Situation of Human Rights in Cuba. Secretary-General (New York): UN, 19 (Nov. 1992): 28 pp.

291. Sklar B. "Cuban Exodus-1980: the Context," *The Political Economy of the Western Hemisphere*,

292. *U.S. Congress*. "Selected Issues for U.S Policy", *Congress of the United States*, 97th Congress, 18 September 1981, First Session, I 842-44.

293. Swanson, R. "Cuba: Revolution Put to the Test" The Political Economy of the Western Hemisphere: Selected Issues, *Congress of the United States*, 97th congress, 18 September 1981, First Session, J 842-44.

294. *Task Force for Indiantown Gap*: After Action Report. 1981, 2 v. :ill., maps: 28cm.

295. *U.S. Congress. House*. Committee on the Judiciary Subcommittee on Courts, Civil Liberties, and the Administration of Justice. Mariel Cuban Detainees U.S. G.P.O: 1989 iv, p. 489 .

296. *United States. Congress*. House. Committee on the Judiciary. Subcommittee on Immigration, Refugees and International Law. Mariel Cuban Detainees U.S. G.P.O., 1989.

Conference Papers

297. Aguila, Juan del. "An Analysis of the Cuban Detainee Population in Atlanta's Federal Penitentiary," Paper presented at the *10th National Meeting of the Latin American Studies Association*, Washington, D.C., March 4-6, 1982.

298. _____. "Occupational and Economic Origins of the New Cuban Refugees," Paper Presented at the *10th National*

Meeting of the Latin American Studies Association, Washington, D.C., March 4-6, 1982.

299. Blackburn, Denise C. "The Cuban-Haitian Influx of 1980: An Operational Perspective," Paper presented at the *Conference of the Center for Migration Studies,* Date and Place Unavailable, 10 pp.

300. Castillo, Siro del. "Cubans of 1980," Paper presented at the *Office of Refugee Resettlement,* Washington, D.C., February 16, 1983, 24 pp.

301. "Conference on the Detention of Mariel Cubans Eight Years After the Boatlift", *SAIS,* February 25, 1988. Washington, D.C., 1988, 53 pp.

302. Darasz, Kathy. "The Economic Adaptation of the Cuban Refugees in Metropolitan Miami," Paper presented at the *International History Honor 'Society Phi Alpha Theta,'* Florida Regional Meeting, University of Florida, Gainesville, February 20, 1982.

303. Díaz-Briquets, Sergio. "The Demographic Context of the Mariel Sealift," Paper presented at the *10th National Meeting of the Latin American Studies Association,* Washington, D.C., March 4-6, 1982.

304. Díaz, Guarioné. "The Truth About the Mariel Refugees," Unpublished paper, *Cuban National Planning Council,* Miami, Florida, 1983.

305. Dixon, Heriberto. "An Overview of the Black Cubans Among the Mariel Entrants," Paper presented at the *Conference on Immigration and the Changing Black Population in the U.S.,* Ann Arbor, Michigan, May 1983.

306. _____. "The Cuban-American Counterpoint: Black Cubans in the United States," Paper presented at the *International Symposium on the Cultural Expression of Hispanics in the United States,* Paris, France, March 12, 1986.

307. Eizenstat, Suart E., and Lisa J. Lubick. "The Mariel Boatlift : A Case Note." Cambridge, MA, *John F. Kennedy School of Government,* Harvard University, 1988.

308. Frisbie, William, Bean Parker, and Frank D. Poston, et al. "Changes in Hispanic Household-Family Structure," Paper available from the *Carolina Population Center, University of North Carolina,* Chapel Hill, North Carolina, 1983.

309. García, María Cristina. "Cuban Exiles and Cuban-Americans: Thirty Years of Defining an Identity and Culture in the U.S." Paper presented at the *XIXth Annual Meeting of the Institute of Cuban Studies*, Orlando, Florida, June 25, 1988.

310. Gonzáles, Diana H. and Clyde B. McCoy. "Cuban Immigration to the U.S.: Is There Any Policy and Research?" Paper presented at the *5th Annual Meetings of the Association for Humanistic Sociology*, Louisville, Kentucky, October 9-12, 1980:12L

311. Guas Inclán, Rosa. "A Report on the Cuban Students in the Dade County Public Schools, Miami, Florida," Working paper for Meeting the Education Needs of Cultural Minorities, *Denver, Colorado, Education Commission of the States*, November 1980.

312. Hernández, Andres and María Rivera. "The Cuban-Haitian Refugee Crisis of 1980: International Context and U.S. Response," Paper presented at the *10th National Meeting of the Latin American Studies Association*, Washington, D.C., March 4-6, 1982.

313. Hernández, Rafael. "Agosto 1980," presented at the Seminario 'Los Mecanismos para la toma de decisión por parte de EE.UU en la formulación de su Política hacia América Latina,' México, 1980.

314. McCoy, Clyde B. and Diana H. Gonzáles. "Policy Implications of Immigration to Florida," Paper read at the *Annual Meeting of the Population Association of America*, March 1981.

315. _____. "Recent Immigration to Florida," School of Medicine, *Department of Psychiatry, University of Miami*, Coral Gables, Florida, No date available.

316. Pérez, John and Bryan O. Walsh. "Report of the Immigrants and Community Relations Panel," Paper for the *Southeast Regional Conference on Immigration and Refugee Issues*, November 1983.

317. Spencer, F., Sazapocnik, K., Santisteban, D., & Rodríguez, A. "Cuban Crisis 1980: Mental Health Care Issues," Presentation at *Southeastern Psychological Association Convention*, Atlanta, Georgia, March 27, 1981.

318. Szapocnik, J. "Trancultural Processes in Mental Health: Concepts Relevant to Cuban Refugees" Presented at *Human*

Services Training Center Symposium, Miami, Florida, March 1981.

Thesis Dissertations

319. Audet, William M. "Representing the Institutionalized Mariel Cubans: the Wisconsin Experience." LL.M. Thesis, University of Wisconsin, Madison, 1987.

320. Bornemann, Thomas Howard. "An Analysis of the Clinical Outcome of a Cohort of Mentally Ill Cuban Entrants from the Mariel Boatlift of 1980." *Dissertation Abstract International,* September, 1993: Vol. 54 (3-B).

321. Canas-Martínez, Jorge E. "The Cuban Immigrant of 1980: An Exploration of Psychological Issues in Migration Experience Through the Topical Life History Method." Ph.D. Dissertation, Boston University, 1984..

322. Colmenero, José Antonio. "Issues and Problems of Cuban Identity and Acculturation." Ph.D. Dissertation, The University of North Carolina at Greensboro, 1985.

323. Engstrom, David Wells. "The Carter Administration's Response to the Mariel Boatlift." Ph.D. Dissertation, University of Chicago, 1992, 2 v.

324. Fradd, Sandra. "Language Acquisition of the Mariel Cuban Immigrants." Ph.D. Dissertation, The University of Florida, 1983.

325. García, María Cristina. "Cuban Exiles and Cuban Americans. A History of an Immigrant Community in South Florida, 1959-89." Ph.D. Dissertation, University of Texas at Austin, 1990.

326. Hidalgo, Olivia Halderman. "Carter, Reagan, and the Cubans: The Impact of Changing Fiscal Policy on Mariel Entrants in Chicago, Illinois." Ph.D. Dissertation, Purdue University, 1986.

327. Lynn, Richard A. "The Mariel Boatlift: a Study in United States Immigration Policies and their Impact on Florida" .M.A. Thesis, Stetson University, 1990.

328. Masud-Piloto, Félix Roberto. "The Political Dynamics of the Cuban Migration to United States, 1959-1980." Ph.D. Dissertation, The Florida State University, 1985.

329. Rich, B. Ruby. "An Evaluative Analysis of the Carter Administration's Policy Toward the Mariel Influx of 1980." Ph.

D. Dissertation, University of Notre Dame, 1983.

330. Torres, María de los Angeles. "From Exiles to Minorities: The Politics of the Cuban Community in the United States," Ph.D. Dissertation, The University of Michigan, 1986.

331. Ugalde, Aileen Maria. "The Mariel Boatlift of 1980: an Examination of the Elements Responsible for its Chaotic Nature." 1988.

Private Report

332. "The Cuban Problem in Perspective, 1958-1980," *The Backgounder*, Heritage Foundation, July 18, 1980: 124.

333. Portes, Alejandro and Juan M. Clark. Los refugiados del Mariel: Seis años después.. *Summary Report Conducted by John Hopkins University and Miami-Dade Community College,* January 1987, 17 pp.

334. Saavedra, V. Reporte Oral 1980; el Caso de la Embajada del Perú y el Mariel Exodo de Cubanos. Washington, D.C.: *Dotación Nacional para las Humanidades,* 1981.

335. Speck, M. "The Cuban Exodus, 1959-1980." Unpublished manuscripts. *American Studies Center,* Standford, California, September 1981.

336. Sullivan, Teresa A., "The Occupational Prestige of Women Immigrants: A Comparison of Cuban and Mexicans," Unpublished paper available at *Carolina Population Center, University of North Carolina,* Chapel Hill, North Carolina, 1983.

Media Listing

337. "Against the Wind and Tide, a Cuban Odyssey". New York, NY: Filmakers Library, 1981 (audiovisual) 1 videocassette (58 minutes).

338. ABC News-Harris Survey "American Uneasy About US Policy Accepting Cuban Refugees." Vol.II, No-64, Survey no. 802114, 16-18 May 1980 (TV-radio-film).

339. "The Cuban Excludables." New York NY: Richter Productions,1994 (audiovisual) 1 videocassette (57 min.) In English and Spanish, with English subtitles.

340. "The Cuban Refugee: One Year Later." 1982, 1981 (audiovisual) 1 videocassette (14 min.)

341. *Dos films de Mariel.* Madrid: Editorial Playor, 1986 (book) 160 pp.

342. Gallup Poll "Immigration to the United States," *Public Opinion*, pp.120-124, Survey 155-G, 5/16-19/89 29 May 1980.

343. Gallup Poll, "Intolerance." *Public Opinion*, Survey 187-G, 11-14/81, (21 January,1981): pp.22.

344. ABC Nightline. "Marielitos: The Forgetten Refugees." July 3, 1987.

345. ABC News-Harris Survey "Negative Feelings Toward Outlaw Refugees." vol.III, no-87, Survey No.802115, 5-9 June 1980.

346. Roblán, Armando "De Colón a Fidel pasando por el Mariel." Miami: *Roblan*, 1980 (recording) 1 sound disc.

347. Milla, J., Ott L. and Villaverde, *M. Films de Mariel. El éxodo cubano de 1980.* Madrid: Editorial Playor, 1980.

Letters, Reports and Microfilm

348. *United Nations. Letter* dated: 16 May 1980 From the Permanent Representative of the United States of America to the United Nations Addressed to the Secretary-General. New York: UN, 20 May 1980. (Issued Under Agenda Item 78. Agenda Document A/35/50.).

349. *United States. Letter,* 22 Jul, Transmitting Communique by Costa Rica Concerning per Sons Who Have Left or are Trying to Leave Cuba (Issued Under Agenda Item 3, Agenda Document E/1980/100).

350. *Cuba. Letter,* 24 Jul. 1980, in Response to E/140/1079 (Issued Under Agenda Item, 3, Agenda Document E/1980/100).

351. *United Nations. Letter* Dated 94/08/22 From the Permanent Representative of Cuba to the United Nations Addressed to the Secretary-General. [New York]: UN, 23 Aug. 1994 (Issued Under Agenda Item 97, Agenda Document A/49/150)..

352. *United Nations. Letter* Dated 94/08/15 From the Charge d'affaires a.i. of the Permanent Mission of Cuba to the United

Nations Addressed to the Secretary-General.[New York]: UN, 16 Aug. 1995.

353. *Cuba*. Issued Under Agenda Item 99, Agenda Document A/49/150. Transmit Report on the Statement Made by the President of Cuba, Fidel Castro, on Cuban Radio and Television on 5 and 11 Aug. 1994 in Connection with Hijacking Cuban Vessels and Cuban Refugees to the United States.

Government Documents

354. Carter, James Earl. "Energy and National Goals." Address to the Nation, July 15 1979. *Public Papers of the Presidents, Jimmy Carter, 1980-1981*, Vol.I. Washington D.C.: Government Printing Office,1981.

355. _____. "League of Women Voters," Remarks and a Question—and Answer Session at the League's Biennal National Convention, May 5, 1980. *Public Papers of the Presidents, Jimmy Carter, 1980-1981*, Vol.I. Washington D.C.: Government Printing Office, 1981.

356. _____. "Address Before the World Council of Philadelphia," May 9, 1980. *Public Papers of the Presidents, Jimmy Carter, 1980-1981*, Vol.I. Washington D.C.: Government Printing Office, 1981.

357. _____. "Cuban Refugees," Remarks to Reporters Announcing Administration Policy Toward the Refugees, May 14, 1980. *Public Papers of the Presidents, Jimmy Carter, 1980-1981*, Vol.I. Washington D.C.: Government Printing Office, 1981.

358. _____. "White House Statement on the Administration Policy Toward the Refugees," May 14, 1980. *Public Papers of the Presidents, Jimmy Carter, 1980-1981*, Vol.2. Washington D.C.: Government Printing Office, 1981.

359. Clinton, William. "The President's News Conference: 19 August, 1994." Weekly Compilation of Presidential Documents, Vol.30, no.33 (22 August 1994), 38-56. New York: *Pathfinder Press*, 1996.

360. Johnson, Lyndon B. "Task Force on the Impact of the Cuban Refugee Program." Letter to the Secretary of Health, Education, and Welfare, November 18, 1965. *Public Papers of*

the Presidents, Lyndon B. Johnson, 1965, Vol. 2. Washington D.C.: Government Printing Office, 1966.

361. Scheina, Robert L. "Coast Guard Operations During the Cuban Exodus." *Washington D.C.: The United States Coast Guard*, 1980.

362. *United States, Army.* Armored Division, 5th. Camp Chaffee, Ark.: rfeveille at the home of the 5th Armored "victory "Division miller ub Co., 1955 1 v. (Unpaged).

363. *United States. Congress. House.* Committee on the Judiciary. Subcommittee on Courts, Civil Liberties, and the Administration of Justice. U.S. G.P.O: 1989 iv, 489 p.

364. *United States. Congress. House.* Committee on the Judiciary. Subcomittee on Immigration, Refugees and International Law. Mariel Cuban detainees.....Washington: U.S. G.P.O., 1989. iii. 148p.

365. *United States. Congress. House.* Committee on the Judiciary. Subcommittee on Courts, Civil Liberties, and the Administration of Justice. Mariel detainess: events preceding and following the Nov.1987 Riots: Hearing before the Subcommitte on Courts, Civil Liberties, and the Administration of Justice of the Committee on the Judiciary, House of Representatives, One Hundreth Congress, Second Session...February 4, 1988. Washington : U.S. G.P.O.: For sale by the Supt. Of Docs., Congressional Sales Office, U.S. G.P.O., 1989 iv, 489.

366. *United States. Dept. Of Justice. Federal Bureau of Prisons.* Federal Detention Center, Oakdale, Louisiana and the U.S. Penitentiary, Atlanta, Georgia Washington D.C. U.S. Dept. Of Justice, Federal Bureau of Prisions, 1988.

367. *U.S. Department of State, Cuban/Haitian Task Force*, Refugiados Cubanos: Last Stop to Freedom, Fort Indiantown Ga, Anville, Pennsylvania: 1980, 8p.

368. *United States, General Accounting Office.* Assesment of Circumstances Leading to the Contract for Comprehensive Mental Health Care Services for Cuban Entrants at Fort Chaffee, Arkansas/ Washington, D.C.: GAO, 1981.

369. *U.S. Congress. House.* Committee on the Judiciary. Subcommittee on Immigration, Refugees, and International Law. Mariel-Cuban Detainees, Hearing July 6, 1988, on the H.R. 4330 and H.R. 4349. Supt. Documents pa 1989.

370. *U.S. Congress. House.* Subcommittee on Immigration, Refugee and International Law. "Caribbean Migration," Hearing Called to Review Cuban Refugee Situation in South Florida. 96th Congress, 2nd. Session, Serial No.84, may 13, June 4,17, 1980. 313 p.

371. *U.S. Library of Congress.* Congressional Research Service. "Refugees in the United States; The Emigration Crisis Summary of the Refugee Act of 1980 with Reference to the Mariel Exodus." Major Legislation of the Congress. Summary Issue 15, 96th Congress, December 1980.

372. *U.S. Senate.* "U.S. Refugee Programs 1981." Hearing Before the Committee on the Judiciary. Washington D.C. : U.S. Government Printing Office, 1980. (Series No. 96-76)

373. Unzueta, Silvia M. Social and Economic Problems Among Cuban and Haitian Entrant Groups in Dade County, Florida: Trends and Indications. Miami. *Fl: Office of County Manager*, 1981.

374. _____. The Mariel Exodus: A Year In Retrospect. Miami, *Fl.: Office of the County Manager*, 1981.

375. *U.S. Presidents. 1980-81. Public Papers of the Presidents of the United States*, Book III. Washington, D.C. : United States Government Printing Office, 1982.

Newspapers (published in the Refugee Camp—Fort Chaffee)

376. *Crossroads.* Fort Chaffee, Ark.: Courier Pub. Co., 1980-1985.

377. *Chaffeegram.* Ft. Chaffee, Ark.: 13th Public Affairs Detachment, Dept. of the Army,1980.

378. *La Vida Nueva.* Fort Chaffee, Ark.: 1st Psyop Bn., Dept. of the Army, 1980-198u.

Popular Journals and Magazines

379. "A Half-Opened Door," *New Republic*, May 24, 1980: 181-5.

380. Alpern, David M. "Carter and the Cuban Influx," *Newsweek*, 1980: 95:22.

381. "And Trouble from Cuban Refugees, Too," *U.S. News and World Report*, August 18, 1980: 89:9.

382. "The Arts: A Boatlift Refugee Rides High," *People Weekly*, Spring 1990:116-119.

383. "Bridging the Cultural Gap," *Time*, November 23, 1981: 118-126.

384. Brogdon, Bill. "Dunkirk 1980," *Boating*, October 1980: 48-68.

385. Burkholz, Herbert. "The Latinization of Miami," *New York Times Magazine*, September 21, 1980: 130:44.

386. "Camp of Fear in Wisconsin," *Time*, September 8, 1980: 116-128.

387. "Carter and the Cuban Influx," *Newsweek*, May 26, 1980: 22-28..

388. "Carter Orders a Cuban Cutoff," *Time*, May 26, 1980: 115-151.

389. Chaze, William L. "Can Miami Cope With New Flood of Refugees?" *U.S. News and World Report*, May 12, 1980: 88:55.

390. _____. "Refugees: Stung by a Backlash," *U.S. News and World Report*, October 13, 1980: 89:60.

391. _____. "In the Last Days of the Cuban Boatlift," *U.S. News and World Report*, June 16, 1980: 88:29.

392. _____. "Dispersing Cubans Easier Said Than Done," *U.S. News and World Report*, June 2, 1980: 88:26.

393. Church, G.J. and R. Woodbury. "Welcome Wears Thin," *Time*, September 1, 1980: 116:8..

394. "The Cuban Exodus," *América*, May 31, 1980: 142:152.

395. "The Cuban Conundrum," *Newsweek*, September 29, 1980: 96:30.

396. "Cuban Castaways," *Nation*, May 30, 1981: 232:652.

397. "Crime Casts Cloud Over Nation's Playground," *U.S. News and World Report*, February 1, 1982: 92-52.

398. Conway, James. "Unwanted Immigrants: Cuban

Prisoners in America," *Atlantic*, February 1981: 247:72.

399. Conner, R. and E.A. McCarthy. "Put Limits on Cuban Refugees?" U.S. *News and World Report*, May 26, 1980: 88:23.

400. Cruz, Amaury. "The Cubans: What Kind of Welcome is This?" *Nuestro*, August 1980: 4:57.

401. "Cold Snap in Miami," *América*, November 22, 1980: 143:319.

402. "Cuban Refugee: Stinging Critique of U.S. Policy," *Time*, September 20, 1982: 120-122.

403. "Cuban Refugees: A Loss Hope," *Newsweek*, March 9, 1981: 87:13.

404. "Cuban Sealift: All in a Day's Work for Coast Guard," U.S. *News and World Report*, June 9, 1980: 88:62.

405. "The Cuban Tide," *Life*, July 1980: 3-35.

406. "Cuba's Boat People-Dilemma for Carter," U.S. *News and World Report*, May 5, 1980: 88:41.

407. "Cuba's Tattered Economy-Through Refugee Eyes," *U.S. News and World Report*, May 26, 1980: 88:21.

408. Daly, Michael. "Los Bandidos Take the Town," *New Yorker*, October 26, 1981:14:67.

409. Demaret, K. "Plagued by Heat, Crime and Snafus, The Fort Chaffee Refugee Camp Becomes a Nightmare," *People*, July 7, 1980: 14:24.

410. "Detention Row," *Progressive*, January 1988: vol.52, no.1, 10.

411. Donzinger, Steven. "INS Treatment of Cubans Offends American Sense of Justice," *Atlanta Journal and Constitution*, November 8, 1987: A1.

412. Dwyer, Timothy. "U.S. Prisons A Limbo For 5,000 Cubans," *Philadelphia Inquirier*, July 13, 1987:A1-4.

413. Ellwood, Wayne. "Share Now or Pay Later," *Macleans*, June 23, 1980: 93:6

414. Engardio, Pete; Javetski, Bill; Weiner, Elizabeth; Pearson, John. "Why the White House Is Finally Warming Up to Havana", *Business Week* (Industrial/Technological Edition), July 4, 1988: 3095:52.

415. "Escape from Paradise," *World Press Review*, June 1980: 27:20.

416. Etzioni, Amitai. "Refugee Resettlement: The Infighting in Washington," *Public Interest*, Fall 1981: 65:15-19.

417. "Exodus Goes On," *Time*, June 2, 1980: 115:21.

418. Ferorelli, Enrico and Jane Cordon. "The New Americans Unprecedented Wave of Immigrants Seek A Better Life Here," *Life*, January 1981: 4:56.

419. "Fleeing from Fidel's Rule: Thousands Beseige the Peruvian Embassy Demanding Asylum," *Time*, April 21, 1980: 115:28.

420. "Florida Tests Cuban, Haitian Parole Status," *Jet*, March 5, 1981: 59;36.

421. "Following in Kennedy's Footsteps: B. Clinton's Feelings About Fidel Castro Go Back to Bay of Pigs Invasion and Mariel Boatlift," *U.S. News and World Report*, September 12, 1994: 117:38.

422. Fonseca, Isabel. "Living in Limbo: Marielitos in Miami," *The Times Literary Supplement*, May 25-31, 1990: 4547:544.

423. "For Most Cubans, U.S. A Happy Haven," *U.S. News and World Report*, September 1, 1980: 89:8.

424. "Freedom Flotilla: A Brave Skipper, A Grateful Family, and Angry Florida Critics," *People Magazine*, May 26, 1980: 13:28.

425. Fuerst, J.S. "Images of Emigres: The U.S. is Never Far Away," *Commonwealth*, July 3, 1981: 108:390.

426. Galbaugh, Glen. "Excludable From Justice," *América*, April , 1987: 156:315.

427. Gormar, M. "Catch 22," *Atlanta Journal*, January 24, 1980: 9:C12.

428. Grudin, Jonathan. "Of Refugees," *New York Times Book Review*, August 10, 1980: 85:33.

429. "Happy To Wash Dishes," *Time*, May 19, 1980: 115:18.

430. Harbron, John. "Strangers in a Strange Land," *Macleans*, May 26, 1980: 93:32.

431. Harris, Marlys. "A New Yanqui Comes Home," *Money*, September 1980: 9:100.

432. "Havana-Bound," *Time*, August 25, 1980: 116:40.

433. Held, Robert. "The Latinization of America: A Growing Minority Portends Cultural Schizophrenia," *World Press Review*, November 1980: 27:45.

434. Hoeffel, P.H. "Fort Chaffee's Unwanted Cubans," *New York Times Magazine*, December 21, 1980: 89:30.

435. "How Open the Arms?" *Forbes*, June 23, 1980: 125:10.

436. Hunt, E. Howard. "Castro's Worms," *National Review*, June 13, 1980: 32:722.

437. "Impatient for Freedom," *Time*, June 16, 1980: 115:29.

438. "In Manhattan's Shadow: A Cuban Enclave of 10,000," *U.S. News and World Report*, October 13, 1980: 89:62.

439. Keerdoga, E. "Cuban Refugees: Limbo in Lima," *Newsweek*, November 2, 1981: 98:22.

440. Kelly, James. "Trouble in Paradise," *Time*, November 23, 1981: 118:22.

441. Kelly, Sheldon. "Midnight Race for Freedom," *Reader's Digest*. September 1989: N 809.

442. Kessler, Jeff. "The Cuban Affair," *World Press Review*, August 1980: 27:16.

443. _____. "Cuban Drama," *World Press Review*, July 1980: 27:14.

444. _____. "Cubans in Miami," *World Press Review*, September 1980: 27:16.

445. Kocheisen, Carol. "Carter Unveils His Policy on Cubans, Haitians," *Nation's Cities Weekly*, June 30, 1980: 3:6.

446. "Land of Opportunity," *Progressive*, July 1982: 46:12.

447. Lang, John S., Joseph L. Galloway, et al. "Castro's Crime Bomb Inside U.S." *U.S. News and World Report*, January 16, 1984: 16:27.

448. Lang, John S. "Castro's Crime Bomb' Inside U.S.: the 1980 Mariel Boatlift Brought Masses of Honest, Hard-Working Cubans to these Shores, but also Criminals and Spies who Plague American Cities,' *U.S. News*, January 16, 1984: 96:27-30.

449. Lanier, Alfredo S. "Give Me Your Tired, Your Poor..." *Chicago*, September 1980: 29:152.

450. "Libre at Last! Libre at Last!" *Time*, September 7, 1981: 118:11.

451. Lowther, William. "And Nobody Waved Goodbye," *Macleans*, May 5, 1980: 93:27.

452. _____. "Despair in the Promised Land," *Macleans*, September 8, 1980: 93:33.

453. _____. "Spy in the Ointment," *Macleans*, April 21, 1981:

93:28.

454. "Lull in Air Hijacking Ends With A Rush," *U.S. News and World Report*, August 25, 1980: 89:8.

455. MacEoin, Gary. "Playing Politics With 'Refugees': How the U.S. Media Distorted the Cuban Exodus," *Progressive*, July 1980: 44:36.

456. Maier, Francis X. and Bruce R. McColm. "Nation in Our Midst: The Cuban Diaspora," *National Review*, February 20, 1981: 33:148.

457. Martenhoff, Jim. "The Freedom Fleet," *Yachting*, July 1980: 148:50.

458. Mayer, Milton. "Massaging the News: UPI Interviews the Huddled Masses," *Progressive*, August 1980: 44.

459. "Mayhem and Murder," *Time*, September 12, 1983: 122:25.

460. McConnell, Malcolm. "Countdown at Talladega: Prison Riot Staged by Marielitos," *Readers' Digest*, June 1992: 140:58-63.

461. McCoy, Clyde B. and Diana H. Gonzales. "Florida's Foreign-Born Population: A Growing Influence on Our Economy," *Business and Economic Dimensions*, 1982: 18: 25-26.

462. McGrath, Ellie; Steven Homes and Robert C. Wurmstedt. "The Cuban Refugees Move On," *Time*, October 13, 1980: 116:45.

463. McGuire, Stryker and Eric Gelman. "The Refugee's Lot," *Newsweek*, May 26, 1980: 95:31.

464. "Men Without a Country," *Newsweek*, June 9, 1986: 29.

465. Menendez, Xavier. "Rescue at Sea," *Nuestro*, November 1980: 4-11.

466. "Miami Recoils," *The Economist*, December 22, 1984: 15-16.

467. "Miami's Agony," *Time*, October 12, 1981: 118:31.

468. "Miami's Army, South Florida is Swamped by Refugee Needs—and Violence," *Time*, October 12, 1981: 31.

469. Michelmore, Peter. "From Cuba With Hate," *Reader's Digest*, December 1982: 121:222.

470. Migdail, Carl J. "Powder Keg at Our Doorstep," *U.S. News and World Report*, May 19, 1980: 88:21.

471. Morganthau, T. and R. Henkoff. "Refugees: Rebels With

A Cause," *Newsweek*, June 16, 1980: 95:28.

472. "New Community Role," *Change*, July/August 1981: 13:29.

473. "New Wave of Cubans is Swamping Miami," *Business Weekly*, August 25, 1980: 86.

474. Nichols, Nick. "Castro's Revenge," *Washington Monthly*, March 1982: 14:38.

475. Nielsen, John. "Cubans Vote With Their Feet," *Newsweek*, April 21, 1980: 95:53.

476. ____. "Flight From Havana," *Newsweek*, April 28, 1980: 95:38.

477. ____. "Sealift from Cuba to Key West," *Newsweek*, May 5, 1980: 95:59.

478. Nielsen, Mark. "Bad Press Creates Difficulties in Resettling Cuban Refugees," *National Catholic Reporter*, August, 15, 1980: 16-22.

479. "No Freedom Yet for Some Cuban Refugees," *U.S. News and World Report*, May 11, 1981: 90:19.

480. "No Haven for the Last of Cuba's Outcasts," *Life*, November 1980: 3:56.

481. Oglesby, J.C.M. "Faltering Revolution Sparks Mass Exodus from Cuba," *International Perspective*, May-June 1980: 33-36.

482. "Open Hearts, Open Arms," *Time*, May 19, 1980: 115:14.,

483. Osborne, John. "Refugees," *New Republic*, September 27, 1980: 183:8.

484. "Out of Cuba and Into Prison," *América*, August 29 and September 5, 1981: 145:82.

485. Page, Clint. "New Orleans Seeks Halt to New Cuban Refugee Project," *Nation's Cities Weekly*, January 24, 1983: 6:3.

486. "Powder Keg: For Cubans Hospitality and Hostility," *U.S. News and World Report*, May 19, 1980: 88:8.

487. Press, Aric. "A Cuban Explosion," *Newsweek*, December 7, 1987: 110:23: 38-43.

488. "Refugee: I Got Here By Faith," *National Catholic Reporter*, September 26, 1980: 16-20.

489. "Refugee Centers to Cost $150 Million Over 2 Years," *Jet*, December 17, 1981: 61:15.

490. "Refugee Gulags," *Nation*, December 12, 1981: 628-629.

491. "Refugee Relief Bill Approved," *Nation's Cities Weekly*, October 6, 1980: 3:8.

492. "Refugee Rights," *Time*, January 12, 1981: 117:52.

493. "Refugee in Florida," *América*, May 17, 1980: 142:414.

494. "Refugees to Puerto Rico," *Nation's Cities Weekly*, October 13, 1980: 3:3.

495. "Resettling Gay Cubans," *Christian Century*, May 6, 1981: 198:504.

496. Russell, Stephanie. "INS Steps Up Deportation Proceedings," *National Catholic Reporter*, March 20, 1981: 17:4.

497. _____. "Sponsor Lack Snarls Life for Cubans Still in Camps," *National Catholic Reporter*, September 26, 1980: 16:1.

498. Sanders, Sol W. "A New Wave of Cubans May Be on the Horizon," *Business Week*, November 16, 1981: 65.

499. "Security Blunts Hijackings; Cuba Spurns Negotiations," *Aviation Week*, August 25, 1980: 113:21.

500. Shabad, Steven. "The Cuban Exodus," *World Press Review*, July 1980: 27:10.

501. _____. "Miami's Travail," *World Press Review*, July 1980: 27:10.

502. Simons, Marlise, "Let Them Go," *GEO*, August, 1980: 2:31.

503. Sloan, Mike. "Slow Tango on a Minefield," *Boating*, August 1980: 48:72.

504. Smith, Vern E. "In the Flotilla at Mariel," *Newsweek*, May 12, 1980: 95:63.

505. Solís, Dianna, and José de Córdoba. "Mariel Firestorm, Cuban Prisoner Riots Followed Seven Years of U.S. Ambivalence; Despite an Initial Welcoming, Many Aliens Are Detained Even After Prison Terms. *Wall Street Journal*, 1987: 210:1+D1.

506. "Start of a Mass Exodus," *Time*, April 28, 1980: 115:32.

507. Taft, A. "Churches Help Absorb New Wave of Refugees," *Church Today*, June 6, 1980: 24:48.

508. Tifft, Susan. "Working Hard Against an Image; For America's Marielitos, the Adjustment Has Been no Easy Trip,"

Time, September 12, 1983: 122:24.

509. Tomlinson, Kenneth Y. "Fleeing Cuba for Freedom," *Reader's Digest*, August 1980: 117:92.

510. "To Send Haitian, Cuban Refugees to Puerto Rico," *Jet*, October 9, 1980: 59:14.

511. "Voyage from Cuba," *Time*, May 5, 1980: 115:42.

512. Vreeland, Leslie N. "This Is the Land of Opportunity," *Money*, Vol.19, N 8, 98, August, 1990: Vol.19, No. 8, 98.

513. Walsh, Bryan O. "The Boat People of South Florida," Americas, May 17, 1980: 142:420.

514. Warner, Edwin. "The Welcome Wears Thin," *Time*, September 1980: 116:8.

515. "War of Refugees," *Nation*, May 17, 1980: 230:577.

516. Wells, S. "Judge Indicates He'll Free Up to 258 Cubans in Pen," *Atlanta Journal*, August 17, 1981: 56:F11.

517. Westfall, Loy Glenn. "Immigrants in Society," *Américas*, July-August, 1982: 34:4.

518. "We Want Out," *Time*, June 9, 1980: 115:23.

519. "We Were Poor in Cuba, but...," *Time*, May 18, 1981: 117:27.

520. "When Cubans Bolt From Refugee Centers," *U.S. News and World Report*, June 9, 1980: 88:13.

521. "Why It's Hard to Cork the Refugee Flow," *U.S. News and World Report*, May 26, 1980: 88:22.

522. "Why 10,000 Cubans Grab Chance to Leave," *U.S. News and World Report*, April 21, 1980: 88:13.

523. Williams, D.A. "Coping With Cuba's Exodus," *Newsweek*, May 12, 1980: 95:60.

524. _____. "Cuban Conundrum," *Newsweek*, September 29, 1980: 95:30.

525. _____. "Cuban Hijackers and Those Who Stay," *Newsweek*, September 1, 1980: 96:26.

526. _____. "Cuban Tide Is A Flood," *Newsweek*, May 19, 1980: 95:28.

527. "With Open Arms," *New Republic*, June 21, 1980: 182:6-8.

528. Womack, John Jr. "The Revolution Tightens Its Belt," *New Republic*, May 31, 1980: 182:19.

529. Woodbury, B. "Escape From Beldlam and Boredom," *Time*, May 12, 1980: 115:38.

530. Woodward, Judith L. "Forgotten, But Not Gone," *Christian Century*, July 15, 1981: 98:724.

531. Wright, Connie. "Cuban Refugees Aren't Really the Riffraff Castro Called Them," *Nation's Cities Weekly*, November 24, 1980: 3:8.

532. Zaldivar, Rayuel Puig. "Freedom to Suffer," *Nuestro*, March 1980: 14-15.

533. Zito, Tom. "Double Dealer: The Cuban Connection," *Rolling Stone Magazine*, September 18, 1980: 43.

General Newspapers Coverage

534. Acuña, Armando and Carl M. Cannon. "Anti-Social Cubans Arriving in San José Area," *San José (Ca.) Mercury*, Thursday, October 15, 1980: 67:C1.

535. "Agradece Carter a Castro la Decisión de Terminar con el Exodo de Cubanos," *Diario Las Américas*, Sunday, September 28, 1980:1.

536. Bagne, Mark. "Five Young Cubans Released to Warmhearted Couple," (Cheyenne) *Wyoming State Tribune*, Tuesday, August 25, 1981: 56:G6.

537. Bancroft, Ann. "Oakland Misled on Refugee Arrival," *Oakland (Ca.) Tribune*, Wednesday, October 14, 1981: 67:B13.

538. Barnes, Fred. "Cecil Base Taken Off List of Likely Refugee Centers," *Baltimore Sun*, Monday, August 10, 1980: 46:F5.

539. Barron, Joan. "Cuban Juveniles Paroled," *Casper (Wyoming) Star Tribune*, Tuesday, August 25, 1981: 56:G9.

540. ____. "Cuban Teen Takes Stand in Cheyenne," *Casper (Wyoming) Star Tribune*, Saturday, August 22, 1981: 56:G10.

541. Bean, G. "Ruling by Appeal Court Offers Hope to Cuban Teens," *Casper Star Tribune*, July 11, 1981: 38:G8.

542. Benjamin, Robert. "Refugees Face Cool Welcome in Baltimore," *Baltimore Sun*, Sunday, May 10, 1981: 26:D9.

543. Benn, Alvin and Peggy Roberson. "Craig Won't Be Site for Cuban Refugees," *Montgomery (Ala.) Advertiser*, Friday, July 10, 1981: 38:F5.

544. "Bill for Cubans Abroad Could Bring Them to Dade," *Miami News*, Friday, April 24, 1987: 5A.

545. Block, Michele. "After Year as Host, Family Wants Cubans Out," *Harford (Conn.) Courant*, Tuesday, September 1, 1981: 56:E7.

546. Brydolf, Carol. "Country Learns of Transfer of Anti-Socials," *Oakland (Calif.) Tribune*, Tuesday, October 13, 1981: 67:B11.

547. "Celebran en Cayo Hueso Aniversario de Mariel," *Diario Las Américas*, Thursday, March 9, 1987: 5B.

548. Chandler, Kurt. "Despite INS Parole Plan, Uncertainty Remains for State's Mariel Cubans," *Minneapolis Star and Tribune*, August 23, 1987: 7B.

549. Clawson, Roger. "Cuban Project Not a Certainty," *Billings (Mont.) Gazette*, Tuesday, June 30, 1981: 38:F10.

550. _____. "Glasgow Warms to Refugee Proposal," *Billings (Mont.) Gazette*, Friday, August 14, 1981: 46:D3.

551. "Clinton's Fidel Problem," *Wall Street Journal*, December 31, 1992: A6.

552. Condon, Tom. "Cubans Finding Help in State," *Hartford (Conn.) Courant*, Monday, May 5, 1980: 20:F3.

553. Craddock, John. "Refugee Here so Glad it is Over," *(Jacksonville) FloridaTimes-Union*, Wednesday, April 30, 1980: 20:G14.

554. Craig, Jim. "Ellington Eyed as Site to Hold Illegal Refugees," *Houston (Tex.) Post*, Saturday, June 13, 1981: 39:B5.

555. _____. "Ellington Won't Become Camp for Refugees," *Houston (Tex.) Post*, Wednesday, July 8, 1981: 38:G2.

556. _____. "Leland Favors Using Ellingston to House Refugees," *Houston (Tex.) Post*, Sunday, June 28, 1981: 38:F11.

557. Crusan, Liz. "Army Says Riots at Fort McCoy Are Unlikely," *(Madison, Wisc.) Capital Times*, Sunday, June 2, 1980: 27:F13.

558. "Cubans at Peruvian Embassy Still on Hunger Strike," *Miami News*, Friday, February 20, 1987: 4a.

559. "Cuban Detention: A Disgrace." *Fulton County Daily Report*, January 30, 1987:1-4.

560. Darnell, Cathy. "Freedom Flotilla Refugees Still Awaiting Settlement Through American Sponsors," *Tennessean*, Wednesday, January 7, 1981: 4:C13.

561. Davis, Ron. "Cecil Official Criticizes Proposed Refugee Transfer After Tour of Ark. Camp," *Baltimore Sun*, Saturday, July 11, 1981: 38:F6.

562. ____. "Cuban Refugees in Arkansas Get Mixed Review at the End," *Baltimore Sun*, Sunday, July 12, 1981: 38:G12.

563. Deener, Bill. "Hope All But Dead for Cubans," *Dallas Morning News*, Sunday August 16, 1981: 46:F10.

564. De La Rosa, Elena O. "Agencies Seek Answers From Each Other in Refugee Death," *Minneapolis Tribune*, Wednesday February 11, 1981: 11:C4.

565. ____. "Hustlers, Survivors, Victims: Truth of Cuban Refugees Resides in the Eye of the Beholder," *Minneapolis Tribune*, Sunday March 8, 1981: 17:B2.

566. ____. "Sponsors Find Themselves Poorly Prepared for Cubans," *Minneapolis Tribune*, Monday March 9, 1981: 17:B10.

567. "Desenvuelven Una Vida Normal en el E.E.U.U. 100,000 Refugiados en la Florida," *Diario Las Américas*, Sunday September 21, 1980: 1.

568. DeWolf, James. "Ex-U.S. Official: Glasgow Too Cold for Latin Refugees," *Billings* (Mont.) *Gazette*, Friday September 4, 1981: 56:F5.

569. ____. "Official Felt at Ease With Cubans," *Billings (Mont.) Gazette*, Saturday September 19, 1981: 56:E14.

570. ____. "U.S. Will Ship Cubans to Glasgow After All," *Billings (Mont.) Gazette*, Friday December 18, 1981: 84:C12.

571. Douthat, Bill. "Austin's Cubans," *(Austin, Tex.) American Stateman*, Sunday June 9, 1980: 27:F2.

572. "Drive For Sponsor of Gay Cuban Refugees Termed a Challenge," *Oakland (Calif.) Tribune*, Sunday July 20, 1980: 34:A13.

573. Drummond, Bob. "Milestone Quietly Reached for Workers at Fort Chaffee," *(Oklahoma City) Daily Oklahoman*, Wednesday July 1, 1981: 39:A1.

574. ____. "3,000 Cuban Refugees Still Waiting at Fort Chaffee for the New Life," *Daily Oklahoman*, Sunday March 29, 1981: 22:C8.

575. Dunson, Lynn and Laura Williams. "Volunteer Agencies Preparing For Influx of Refugees," *Washington (D.C.) Star*, Friday May 24, 1980, 27:F9.

576. "Duró Una Hora la reunión de Castro con McHenry," *Diario Las Américas*, Sunday July 20: 1A.

577. Eagan, Margery. "Most Cubans Settle In," *(Boston, Mass.) Herald American*, Tuesday September 22, 1981, Social Relations 57:A9

578. Elich, Patricia. "Will Glasgow Become Next Ellis Island," *Billings (Mont.) Gazette*, Thursday July 30, 1981: 46:F6.

579. "Exile Boats Arrive Near Havana," *Miami News*, Monday April 21, 1980: 1A.

580. Fanlund, Paul and Susan Kepecs. "Police Wary of Cubans," *(Madison, Wisc.) State Tribune*, Sunday September 13, 1981: 57:A12.

581. _____. "Small Group of Cubans Causes Trouble for Many," *(Madison, Wisc.) State Tribune*, Sunday September 13, 1981: 57:A13.

582. Flinchum, James M. "Cuban Teenager Wants to Stay in America," *Wyoming State Tribune*, Monday August 4, 1981: 56:G7.

583. _____. "Legal Battle Over Teens to Resume Here Monday," *Wyoming State Tribune*, Saturday August 22, 1981: 56:G11.

584. "Forty-Four Mariels Moved From Krome to Texas," *Miami News*, Saturday March 7, 1987: 15A.

585. Foster-Pegg, Perri. "Cubans: A Cause, A Crisis," *Trenton (N.J.)Times*, Sunday July 27, 1980: 34:C8.

586. Gailey, Phil. "Carter Asks Speed-up of Processing," *Washington (D.C.) Star*, Monday June 3, 1980: 27:F6.

587. Gandleman, Joe. "Cubans Find Image of U.S. Just a Dream," *Wichita (Kan.) Eagle*, Monday October 19, 1981: 67:C3.

588. Garcia, Philip. "Scrambled Boatlift Left Future of Thousands Floating," *Arizona Daily Star*, Sunday February 8, 1981: 11:B12.

589. Gerbert, Armand. "Life Tough for Cubans in Detroit," *The Detroit News*, Sunday February 19, 1984: 1B.

590. _____. "Refugees Ask for a Job and a Green Card," *The Detroit News*, Sunday February 19, 1984: 1B.

591. Golden, Daniel. "U.S. No Haven for These Cuban Refugees," *Boston Globe*, March 29, 1987: A23-26.

592. "Group Says Cuban Revolutionaries Infiltrated With

Refugees," *Washington (D.C.) Star*, Friday February 13, 1981: 3A.

593. Guillén, Tomás. "Cuban Prisoners' Chance for Asylum: Slim and None," *Seattle (Wash.) Times*, Sunday June 29, 1980: 34:C12.

594. _____. "Cubans at McNeil to Get Help From Bar Association," *Seattle (Wash.) Times*, Thursday June 17, 1980: 34:D1.

595. _____. "Frustration: Why Won't You Believe Us? Cubans Ask Sadly," *Seattle (Wash.) Times*, Friday July 4, 1980: 34:D2.

596. Hanners, David. "Cuban Refugees Unwanted, Texans Say," *Dallas Morning News*, Wednesday July 22, 1981: 46:D5.

597. Harwood, John. "Smith: Florida to Get Immigration Help Soon," *St. Petersburg (Fla.) Times*, Sunday June 28, 1981: 38:G5.

598. Henriques, Diana. "Gradually, Cuban Refugees Adjust to New Lives in the U.S.," *Trenton (N.J.) Times*, Sunday August 2, 1981: 46:F13.

599. Hensel, Pat. "Cuban's Journey is Far From Over," *(Madison, Wisc.) State Journal*, Sunday March 15, 1981: 17:B8.

600. _____. "Image is Cubans' Problem," *Milwaukee Journal*, Monday April 27, 1981: 26:D12.

601. Herbut, Paula. "Underground Religion Offers Refuge for the Frightened," *(Philadelphia, Penn.) Evening Bulletin*, Sunday August 16, 1981: 62:D3.

602. Hernández, María. "Cubans Thriving in New Denver Life," *Denver Post*, Saturday May 25, 1980: 20:F1.

603. Hilman, Randy. "Idle Cubans Wait and Wonder," *Tennessean*, Thursday April 30, 1981: 26:D11.

604. Hoefling, Larry and Denise Gamino. "McAlester in Running for New Federal Deportation Center," *Daily Oklahoman*, Wednesday August 12, 1981, 46:F7.

605. Hopkins, Sam. "Feds Release 17 Cubans: 1,800 Wait," *Atlanta Journal*, Saturday August 22, 1981: 56:F13.

606. _____. "Hearings Slated for 1,800 Jailed Cubans," *Atlanta Journal*, Saturday August 8, 1981: 56:F8.

607. "In a Strained Miami, Cubans and Haitians Help the

Boat People," *Wall Street Journal*, Friday May 2, 1980: 1.

608. "'Inflammatory' Articles producer to Shun Miami as Movie Site," *Associated Press*, *Orlando Sentinel*, August 31, 1982: B6.

609. Jolin, Bill. "Refugees Tell of Hardship, Deprivations," (Portland) *Oregonian*, Sunday January 11, 1981: 4:C3.

610. "Judge Orders Refugee's Release," *The Los Angeles Daily Journal*, April 24, 1981: 3.

611. Katz, Jeffrey. "Days Slow for Cubans at Chaffee," (Memphis, Tenn.) *Commercial Appeal*, Sunday May 18, 1980: 20:E11.

612. Kavanaugh, Kevan. "Cubans Wanting to Sink Roots Find Social Climate a Bit Frosty," *St. Paul Pioneer Press*, Sunday July 26, 1981: 46:F11.

613. Kepecs, Susan. "Cuban Job-Hunters Hurt by Violence," (Madison, Wisc.) *State Journal*, Sunday September 13, 1981: 57:B2.

614. Kneece, Jack. "Port Isabel Studied for Housing Cubans," *Dallas Morning News*, Wednesday July 23, 1981: 46:F9.

615. Knoble, John. "Jehovah's Witnesses Aid Their Own Amid Cuban Exodus," *New Haven (Conn.) Register*, Sunday July 13, 1980: 34:B5.

616. Kole, John W. "Care Urged on Refugee Spending," *Milwaukee Journal*, Sunday July 19, 1981: 38:F4.

617. Kunstel, Marcia. "ACLU Fights Forced Food for Inmate," *Atlanta Journal*, Friday May 22, 1981: 26:F4.

618. _____. "Anger Fill Those Who Still Await Release,' *Atlanta Journal*, Thursday August 20, 1981: 26:D13.

619. _____. "Cubans Again Ask Court Ban On Pen Brutality," *Atlanta Journal*, Wednesday June 3, 1981: 31:A6.

620. _____. "Cubans in Pen Still on Hunger Strike," *Atlanta Journal*, Wednesday May 20, 1981: 26:D14.

621. _____. "First Detainee's Release Bolsters Hopes for Other Cubans Still in Pen," *Atlanta Journal*, Friday June 12, 1981: 26:D14.

622. _____. "Judge Assails Plan to Process Cubans," *Atlanta Journal*, Sunday July 23, 1981: 46:E3.

623. _____. "Judge May Act Soon to Free up to 300 Cubans From Pen," *Atlanta Journal*, Friday July 24, 1981: 46:E5.

624. ____. "Judge Orders Cuban Set Free by Noon Friday," *Atlanta Journal*, Thursday June 4, 1981: 38:G9.

625. ____. "17 Cuban Detainees Going Free," *Atlanta Journal*, Friday August 21, 1981: 56:F12.

626. ____. "Florida Will Fight Release of Cubans," *Atlanta Journal*, Tuesday August 25, 1981: 56:G4.

627. Larsen, Kim. "Bad Luck Haunts Cuban Exiles," *Billings (Mont.) Gazette*, Thursday September 17, 1981: 57:A10.

628. ____. "Cubans' Plight Eased by Aid from Readers," *Billings (Mont.) Gazette*, Friday September 18, 1981: 57:A11.

629. "Little by Little, Cubans Learn American Way," *Tallahassee (Fla.) Democrat*, Saturday June 8, 1980: 34:C1.

630. Lowerstein, Roger. "Miami Vise: The Herald is Wooing Cuban Readers, but it Risks Loss of Anglos," *The Wall Street Journal*, March 5, 1987:1.

631. McMahon, Patrick. "Emergency Declared Over Cuban Refugees," *St. Petersburg Times*, Tuesday April 29, 1980: 20:F5.

632. McNulty, Bryan. "Local Refugees Family Sought Liberty," Portland (Me.) *Press Herald*, Monday January 12, 1981: 4:D1.

633. Manson, Pamela. "Cuban Refugees Complain They Must Live in the Streets," *Arizona Republic*, Monday July 20, 1981: 46:F12.

634. Martin, Victoria. "Cubans Arriving in Portland Finding Begrudging Refuge," *Oregonian*, Sunday January 11, 1981: 4:C5.

635. —. "Oregon Life Harsh for Cuban Refugees," *Oregonian*, Sunday January 11, 1981: 4:C7.

636. Martindale, Rob. "Despair Fills Cubans' Lives at Chaffee," *Tulsa (Okla.) World*, Sunday August 9, 1981: 46:D7.

637. Miller, Marjorie. "Cuban Refugees Find Disillusionment in New Land," *San Jose Mercury*, Sunday August 30, 1981: 57:A6.

638. Moore, Jeanne. "Death of a Refugee," *St. Louis Globe-Democrat*, Monday July 13, 1981: 38:F1.

639. Nazario, Sonia. "Cubans Jailed in U.S. Start a Court Fight," *Wall Street Journal*, Friday January 21, 1983:1.

640. "Negocios de los Communistas en Mariel," *Diario Las Américas*, Thursday May 8, 1980:16B.

641. "New Look at 'Marielitos': Latest Report," *Miami News*, Saturday March 7, 1987: 3V.

642. Oberdorfer, Dan. "Cubans Jeered at Winona Priority," *Minneapolis Tribune*, Wednesday May 13, 1981: 26:E6.

643. _____. "Hostile Response Ends Plan for 5 Cuban Centers," *Minneapolis Tribune*, Wednesday May 27, 1981: 31:A12.

644. _____. "Plan to Move Cubans to Winona Area is Opposed," *Minneapolis Tribune*, Tuesday May 12, 1981: 26:E5.

645. _____. "Plan to Resettle Cubans in Winona Dropped," *Minneapolis Tribune*, Tuesday June 2, 1981: 31:A8.

646. _____. "2 State Cuban Resettlement Plans in Jeopardy," *Minneapolis Tribune*, Thursday May 14, 1981: 26:E3.

647. _____. "Waiting Game Confuses Cubans Resettling in Winona," *Minneapolis Tribune*, Thursday May 28, 1981: 31: A13.

648. "Obligan a una Cubana a recorrer las calles de La Habana con un cartel infamante colgado del cuello," *Diario Las Américas*, Thursday May 22, 1980:10A.

649. "Officials Again Delay Closing Refugee Center at Fort Chaffee," *Daily Oklahoman*, Saturday September 5, 1981: 56:F1.

650. O'Leary, Jeremiah. "Florida Declared Disaster Area, $10 Million Allotted for Refugees," *Washington (D.C.) Star*, 20:D4.

651. Palomo, Juan Ramón. "Many Residents Fearful of Detention Center Plan," *Houston Post*, Sunday June 21, 1981: 38:F14.

652. Payne, Karen and Paul Fonteboa. "U.S. is Moving to Grant Mariel Cubans Residency," *Miami News*, Thursday October 18, 1984: 1A.

653. Pérez, Miguel. "Cuban Tide Swamps Local Refugee Facilities," *New York Daily News*, Tuesday July 22, 1980: 34:C10.

654. Pope, John. "Five in 'Freedom Flotilla' Will Go On Trial Today," *New Orleans Times-Picayune*, Monday November 9, 1981: 76:E3.

655. _____. "On Trial: Flotilla Priests to Confront Critics," *New Orleans-Picayune*, Sunday November 8, 1981: 76:E1.

656. ____. "Priest Blasts New Charges Over Boatlift," *New Orleans Times-Picayune*, Wednesday August 26, 1981: 56:E9.

657. ____. "Producer: Priests Paid $18,000 for Film," *New Orleans Times-Picayune*, Saturday November 14, 1981: 76:E6.

658. ____. "Refugees Tell of Harassment Before Boatlift," *New Orleans Times-Picayune*, Wednesday November 18, 1981: 76:D9.

659. ____. "Trial Was Clergy vs. Carter Staff, Fed-up Florida," *New Orleans Times-Picayune*, Sunday November 22, 1981: 84:B12.

660. ____. "What Did the Priests Know and When?" *New Orleans Times Picayune*, Monday November 16, 1981: 76:D13.

661. ____. "You Have to Go Ahead with it, Rep. Long Says He Advised Priest," *New Orleans Times-Picayune*, Tuesday November 17, 1981: 76:D13.

662. Poque, John. "Last Stop Philadelphia for the Refugees Nobody Wanted," *Philadelphia Inquirer*, Sunday June 28, 1981: 39:A4.

663. "Prison Saves Oakdale, La., Improves Mariels Lives," *Miami News*, Monday May 18, 1986:7A.

664. Raffensperger, Gene. "Cuban Boat People Still Feel Adrift in Iowa," *Des Moines (Iowa) Register*, Sunday November 1, 1981: 56:F2.

665. "Refugiados de Mariel y Su Integración," *Diario Las Américas*, Wednesday January 14, 1987:1B.

666. Reid, Kenneth. "New Challenger for Little Havana," *(Newark, N.J.) Star-Ledger*, Sunday March 1, 1981: 17:B6.

667. Rodríguez, Don. "Cuban Refugee Begin a Delayed Life of Freedom," *Kansas City Star*, Sunday August 9, 1981: 46:E2.

668. Rummler, Gary C. "Refugees Share Efforts to Adapt," *Milwaukee Journal*, Tuesday January 27, 1981: 11:D5.

669. Salvia, Joe. "Two Young Cubans Sue Detention Center," *St. Louis Globe-Democrat*, Saturday-Sunday August 15-6, 1981: 46:E13.

670. Sayles, Frank Jr. "Cuban Refugees in Area Seeking Employment," *(Charleston, S.C.) News and Courier*, Sunday January 11, 1981: 4:C11.

671. Schjonberg, Mary Frances. "Cuban Refugees Seeking Niche in American Society," *(Madison, Wisc.) State Journal,* Sunday April 5, 1981: 22:C14.

672. Schultz, Rick. "Glasgow Project Boss Quits," *Billings (Mont.)Gazette,* Friday July 17, 1981: 38:F3.

673. Sikora, Frank and R.E. Hogan. "Cubans at Talladega Say They Were Deported As State Enemies," *Birmingham (Ala.) News,* Thursday May 8, 1980: 20:D8.

674. Simms, Patricia. "Cuban's Month at Camp Cost $7,700 Each," *(Madison , Wisc.) State Journal,* Sunday March 29, 1981: 17: A14.

675. "Simpson Says Dead Bill Will Mean Less Hispanic Hiring," *Miami News,* Wednesday August 8, 1984: 4A.

676. Sitter, Albert J. "Valley Has Become Stopping Place for Cuban Criminals, Official Claim," *Arizona Republic,* Friday September 11, 1984: 56:F6.

677. Skiptares, Connie. "No More 'Anti-Social' Cubans Coming Here," *San José Mercury,* Tuesday November 3, 1981: 76:E13.

678. Smith, C. Fraser and Edna Goldberg. "Cecil Site Considered for Refugees," *Baltimore Sun,* Thursday July 9, 1981: 38:F8.

679. Spencer, Richard. "Gay Cuban Resettlement Plan," *Oakland Tribune,* Thursday July 3, 1980: 34:A12.

680. "Study: Economic Outlook for Mariels Has Improved,' *Miami News,* Monday January 12, 1987: 5A.

681. Treadway, Joan. "Alien Mission," *New Orleans Times-Picayune,* Saturday June 13, 1981: 31:A5.

682. _____. "N.O. Opposes Program to Resettle, Train Refugees," *New Orleans Times-Picayune,* April 18, 1983: 15:B8.

683. "U.S. to Release 14 Cubans Held in New York Jail," *The Los Angeles Daily Journal,* December 1, 1980:29.

684. Usabel, Gaizka. "Refugees Face Months of Training-But They're Willing," *(Madison, Wisc.) Capital Times,* Thursday May 30, 1980: 27:G6.

685. Warren, Bill. "Graham Lashes U.S. for State's Refugee Troubles," *Florida Times-Union,* January 13, 1981: 4:C2.

686. Watt, Joe. "Refugees in Denver After Wyo. Protest," *Denver Post,* Friday June 19, 1981: 31:B3.

687. Wells, Susan. "Court Ruling May Be Major Obstacles to Cubans' Release from Penitentiary," *Atlanta Journal*, Wednesday November 18, 1981: 76:E10.

688. ____. "Cubans Sue Over Condition in Pen," *Atlanta Journal*, Thursday February 12, 1981: 11:B9.

689. ____. "Judge Halts Deportation of Cubans," *Atlanta Journal*, Thursday August 20, 1981: 46:D11.

690. ____. "Judge Indicates He'll Free Up to 258 Cubans in Pen," *Atlanta Journal*, Monday August 17, 1981: 56:F11.

691. ____. "Mayor Urges U.S. Plan for Freed Cubans," *Atlanta Journal*, Tuesday August 18, 1981: 56:F14.

692. ____. "1,800 Cubans at Pen Here Seeking Refugee Status," *Atlanta Journal*, Friday July 10, 1981: 38:F13.

693. ____. "Release of Cubans May Begin With 90," *Atlanta Journal*, Wednesday August 19, 1981: 46:D9.

694. ____. "Shoob Puts the U.S. on Trial, Forces Solution on Jailed Cubans," *Atlanta Journal*, Sunday August 23, 1981: 56:G2.

695. ____. "U.S. Asks Delay in Cuban Release," *Atlanta Journal*, Saturday August 21, 1981: 46:D13.

696. ____. "U.S. Challenges Order Barring Cubans' Return," *Atlanta Journal*, Wednesday November 4, 1981: 76:E12.

697. Wells, Susan and Tracy Wilkinson. "Cubans in Atlanta Pen Stymie Officials," *Atlanta Journal*, Sunday February 8, 1981: 11:B13.

698. Wenzl, Roy. "Restlessness, Uncertainty Gnaw at Cuban Prisoners," *Kansas City Star*, Tuesday July 15, 1980: 34:C6.

699. Whitefield, Mimi. "Cuba Recalls Boatlift with Selective Memory," *The Houston Chronicle*, April 1, 1990: 25A.

700. Wier, Patrick. "Jury Charges INs Guards With Beating," *El Paso (Tex.) Times*, Thursday October 8, 1983: 67:C5.

701. Woolf, Jim. "Expert Urges Cuts in Refugee Aid," *Salt Lake Tribune*, Monday July 6, 1981: 38:G4.

702. Zimmerman, Richard G. "Parolee Refugees Left to Find Own Way in U.S.," *(Cleveland, Ohio) Plain Dealer*, Sunday July 6, 1980: 34:B8.

703. ____. "The U.S. Immigration Mess," *(Cleveland, Ohio) Plain Dealer*, Friday July 4, 1980: 34:A9.

704. Zurawik, Dave. "16 Cuban Refugees Moved to Detroit," *Detroit Free Press*, Thursday February 19, 1981: 11:C12.

Newspapers

Chicago Tribune

705. "...And Some Prod Cubans to Move On," Monday, May 5, 1980: 1.

706. "Boatlift Brings 450 Cubans Despite Ban," Thursday, April 24, 1980:3.

707. "Boats Carry Cuban Refugees to U.S.," Tuesday, April 22, 1980:3.

708. "Catholic Groups Work for Release of More Cubans," Thursday, January 29, 1987:5.

709. "Carter Orders Vessels to Divert to Aid Fleeing Cubans," Thursday, May 1, 1980:1.

710. "Carter to Deport Cuban Criminals," Thursday, June 5, 1980:7.

711. "Castro Halts Costa Rica Flights," Saturday, April 9, 1980:3.

712. Coakley, Michael. "3,500 Cubans Get U.S. Asylum," Tuesday, April 15, 1980:8.

713. "Costa Rica Offers to Take All Refugees Leaving Cuba," Monday, April 21, 1980:2.

714. "Cuba Sea Exodus in Chaos," Tuesday, April 29, 1980:1.

715. "Cuban Exiles Must Register for the Draft," Friday, September 12, 1980:1.

716. "Cuban Refugee Camp Not Full of Mentally Ill, Doctors Say," Thursday, September 18, 1980: 11.

717. "Cubans Empty Prison For Sealift," Thursday, June 5, 1980:7.

718. "Cubans Jam Camps; Food Runs Short," Thursday, May 8, 1980:2.

719. "High Court Oks Refugee Shift to Puerto Rico," November 4, 1980:10.

720. Keegan, Anne. "All the Ft. McCoy Cubans Want is Freedom," Monday, June 9, 1980:5.

721. _____. "It's Preferable to Die at Sea Than Live in Cuba," Sunday, June 1, 1980:1.

722. _____. "The Train to Freedom Stalls as Refugees Seek Sponsors," Tuesday, August 5, 1980:1.

723. Lama, George de. "Camp Has Tranquil Look," Sunday, September 28, 1980:5.

724. ____. "Castro Uses Refugees to Twist U.S. Tail," Wednesday May 7, 1980:16.

725. ____. "Cubans Here Greet 14 Who Fled Castro," Wednesday, May 21, 1980:14.

726. ____. "For Cuban Teens, Tent City is a Small Heaven," Thursday, May 8, 1980:1.

727. ____. "Ft. McCoy a Timebomb Just Waiting to Blow," Sunday, September 7, 1980:1.

728. ____. "Life in U.S. for Two Refugees: To One Horror, The Other Hope," Monday, October 6, 1980: 2.

729. ____. "Mood Over Miami: Cubans' Concern for Countrymen," Sunday, April 13, 1980:8.

730. ____. "No Welcome Mat for Refugees in Puerto Rico," Sunday, September 28, 1980:5.

731. ____. "Olive-Drab Blues Afflicts Refugees Arriving in U.S.,"Thursday, May 15, 1980:5.

732. ____. "Puerto Rico Opposed to Cuban Influx," Thursday, September 25, 1980:14.

733. ____. "Refugee Sealift is Halted by Cuba," Saturday, September 27, 1980:2.

734. ____. "Some Refugee Vignettes From Reporters Notes," Sunday, May 18, 1980:12.

735. Lama, George de, and Charles Madigan. "GI's Turning Ft. Chaffee Into Prison for Cubans," Sunday, September 14, 1980:6.

736. Lyon, Jeff. "Cuban Refugees: Update on latest 'huddled masses'," February 11, 1981: 11: C10.

737. ____. "If This is Slavery, Cubans Want More of it," Friday, May 2, 1980: 1.

738. Maclean, John. "Report U.S. Will Send Cubans to Puerto Rico,"Tuesday, September 23, 1980:1.

739. Maclean, John and Michael Sneed. "Senators to Study Influx of Cubans," Sunday September 14, 1980:6.

740. Madigan, Charles. "Frustration Growing in Other Miami: Blacks Feel Threatened by Influx of Cubans," Wednesday, July 2, 1980:1.

741. Oppenheim, Carol. "Cuban Exile Hits Policy on Castro," Monday, September 15, 1980:1.

742. "Peru Prepares to Move 10,000 Cuban Refugees," Saturday, April 21, 1980:19.

743. "Record Number of Refugees Arrive in South Florida," Monday, May 5, 1980:1.

744. "Refugees Sue Over Welfare," Friday, July 25, 1980: 1.

745. "Sealift Boats Filled With Undesirables," Monday, June 9, 1980:6.

746. "10,000 Throng Embassy Seeking to Leave Cuba," Monday, 17, 1980:1.

747. "Transfers to Ft. Chaffee Set," Thursday, September 25, 1980:14.

748. "217 Refugees Leave Cuba With Happy Heart in Boat," Wednesday, April 23, 1980:3.

749. "236 Cubans Take Flight to Freedom," Thursday, April 17, 1980:2.

750. "U.S. Will Accept 600 More Cubans," Friday, October 17, 1980:8.

751. Weidrich, Bob. "The Refugees, A U.S. Disgrace," Friday, May 30, 1980: 3.

Christian Science Monitor

752. "ACLU Files Human Rights Petition With OAS For Atlanta Cubans," Friday, April 17, 1987:2.

753. "Act Now on Immigration," Tuesday, August 17, 1982:24.

754. "Arkansas Appeal on Refugees," Wednesday, September 3, 1980:24.

755. "Boatlift Brings Cubans to U.S.," Thursday, April 24, 1980:8.

756. Dillin, John. "Congress Wants to Drive Hard Bargain Over Cuban POWs," Wednesday, November 2, 1983:3.

757. Drummond, Roscoe. "If Castro Falls What Next?" Wednesday, June 9, 1982:3.

758. Germani, Clara. "Who Shoulders the Refuge Burden?" Wednesday, June 9, 1982:3.

759. Grier, Peter. "U.S. Politicians Court Hispanics But Come Bearing Few Gifts," Monday, April 30, 1984:1.

760. Godsell, Geoffrey. "Cuba's Refugee 'Dunkirk': Castro Hopes it Will Embarrass the U.S." Friday, April 25, 1980:1.

761. _____. "It's Happening Again: Cubans Flee in Search of Better Life," Monday, April 7, 1980:1.

762. Goodsell, James Nelson. "Castro Smoothly Turns Refugee Exodus to Political Advantage," Tuesday, May 27, 1980:11.

763. "Inside Report: Almost a Year After Their Arrival Here, Nearly 6,000 Cuban Refugees Are Still Not Settled," Friday, March 13, 1981:2.

764. Klein, Gil. "Majority of Cuban Refugees Work Hard to Get Ahead, Contradict Bad Image," Wednesday, May 18, 1983:4.

765. Malone,Julia. "Hispanic Political Pressure Stops Immigration Reform in Congress,"Thursday, October 6, 1983:4.

766. _____. "Immigration Reform Nearer," Friday, May 20, 1983:1.

767. _____. "Speaker O'Neil Opens House Door to Immigration Reform," Monday, December 5, 1983:3.

768. "New Cuban Influx on the Horizon," Tuesday, May 24, 1980:2.

769. Press, Robert M. "Cuban Flotilla Ending as Total Nears 100,000," Tuesday, June 3, 1980:1.

770. _____. "Cuban Flotilla to U.S. is Back in Business," Wednesday, July 30, 1980:4.

771. _____. "Federal Courts Open Prison Doors to Free 'Nondangerous' Cubans," Wednesday, August 19, 1981:4.

772. _____. "Haiti 'Boat People' Find no Anchor in U.S.," Friday, May 2, 1980:3.

773. _____. "Hunger Strike Dramatizes Plight of Cuban Detainees," Wednesday, May 20, 1981:6.

774. _____. "If Cubans Are Sent Back, Would They Face Persecution?" Friday, May 16, 1980:3.

775. _____. "Most Cuban Refugee On Way Up," Tuesday, November 4, 1980:1.

776. _____. "Why Cuban Refugees Are Fleeing Castro's Island," Thursday, May 15, 1980:1.

777. "Probe Death of Mariel in Atlanta," Tuesday, April 21, 1987:6.

778. Strout, Robert L. "Controversial Reform Gets New Hearing in Washington," Tuesday, March 1, 1983:3.

779. _____. "Cuban 'Boatlift' to Florida Spotlights Ambiguous U.S. Immigration Policy," Monday, May 5, 1980.

780. _____. "Immigration Reform Back on the Agenda," Friday, April 8, 1983:3.

781. "U.S. Announces Plan to Cut South Florida Refugee Flow," Friday, September 19, 1980:2.

782. "U.S. House Approves Funds for Refugees," Monday, December 15, 1980:2.

783. "U.S. Offers $1,000 Grants to Resettle Cubans," Tuesday, October 21, 1980:2.

784. Webbe, Stephen. "Coast Guard Sheepherding Cubans from Danger to Succor," Thursday, May 8, 1980:3.

785. _____. "Refugee Tide: Little Sign of Ebbing," Monday, May 12, 1980:1.

786. Yemma, John. "Refugees, Refugees, Refugees," Wednesday, May 28, 1980:5.

787. _____. "U.S. Response to Cuban Tide 'Impressive' in Retrospect," Friday, June 6, 1980:4.

788. _____. "White House Spells Out Its 'Open Arms' Policy as Political, Social Pressures Grow," Thursday, May 14, 1980:1.

789. "You Remember Simpson Mazzoli, Don't You? Don't You?" Thursday, April 28, 1983:24.

Miami Herald

790. "Alien Limbo," Monday, March 5, 1985:18A.

791. "A Way Out for INS," Thursday, February 16, 1984:30A.

792. "Avoid New Mariel, Revive Legal Cuban Migration," Thursday, May 28, 1987:23A.

793. Anderson,Paul. "Amnesty: The Toughest Question in Alien Immigration Legislation,"Sunday, June 17, 1984:1A.

794. _____. "Audit: Refugee Resettlement Fine, But Return $195,749," Saturday, May 19, 1984:16A.

795. _____. "Bill Would Settle Refugees' Status," Friday, February 10, 1984:1A.

796. _____. "Decision on Mariel Status is Tentative," Monday, February 13, 1984:1A.

797. _____. "Floridians Help Shape New Immigration Bill," Sunday, June 17, 1984:20A.

798. _____. "Health Cards for Aliens Rejected," Tuesday,

February 9, 1982:8.

799. ____. "Here is How Alien Bill Would Work," Friday, June 22, 1984:1A.

800. ____. "Hispanics Unite on Immigration," Thursday, February 2, 1984:2A.

801. ____. "House Bill on Aliens in Trouble," Thursday, July 26, 1984:1A.

802. ____. "House Erases Rules on Foreign Workers," Friday, June 15, 1984:1A.

803. ____. "House OKs Fines for Hiring Illegal Aliens," Thursday, June 14, 1984:1A.

804. ____. "Immigration Bill is Still Stalled on Anti-discrimination Section," Thursday, September 27, 1984:2A.

805. ____. "Immigration Compromise Break Down Over a Clause," Thursday, September 20, 1984:7A.

806. ____. "Immigration Conferees Debate Alien Benefits," Friday, September 21, 1984:11A.

807. ____. "INS Chief Supports Cubans, Haitians on Residents Status," Thursday, May 10, 1984:12A.

808. ____. "Mariel Refugee Lived at D.C. Zoo," Tuesday, March 13, 1984:1A.

809. ____. "Measure to Give Refugees Legal Status Dead Until '85," Friday, October 12, 1984:5A.

810. ____. "Stalled Immigration Bill Gets New Push," Sunday, February 26, 1984:14A.

811. "Another 80 Set to Leave Fort Chaffee," Monday, January 25, 1982:13A.

812. Arocha, Zita. "Crime With A Marielito Accent Has Come to Broward, Too," Sunday, February 7, 1982:7B

813. ____. "Mariels Scorned," Monday, March 23, 1981:2B.

814. ____. "Tatoo May (or May Not) Tell Refugee's Claim to Notoriety," Sunday, February 7, 1982:7B.

815. "As Boatlift Wanes, Castro Sends Hundreds of Criminals," Thursday, June 5, 1980: 1A.

816. Balmaseda, Liz. "After Two Decades, United States is Closing 'Open Door' to Cubans," Saturday, November 21, 1981:1A.

817. ____. "Chaffee: Politics at Expense of Helpless," Sunday, January 31, 1982:1A.

818. ____. "Mariel Misfits Face Deportation for Crimes

Here," Tuesday, December 25, 1984:1A.

819. _____. "Marielito is Not a Dirty Word," November 1, 1981: 1G, 6G.

820. _____. "Red Tape Slows Relocation of Frustrated Mariel Refugees," Friday, March 20, 1981:5B.

821. _____. "Refugees One Cause of Flight," Friday, April 23, 1982:18A.

822. _____. "U.S. Unveils Residency Plan for 100,000 Mariel Refugees," Tuesday, November 20, 1984:1A.

823. Balmaseda, Liz and Nery Ynclan. "Last Cubans Leave Chaffee for Chicago," Friday, February 5, 1982:20A.

824. Beck, Joan. "Simpson Mazzolli Bill is A Beginning," Tuesday, June 19, 1984:17A.

825. "Blockade Fails to Stop 276 Foot Cruise Liner," Tuesday, June 3, 1980: 16A.

826. Bohning, Don. "Fidel Turns Embarrassment Into Advantage," Sunday, April 27, 1980:1A.

827. _____. "Legal Cuban Entries Virtually at Standstill," Saturday, September 12, 1981: 26A.

828. _____. "U.S. Won't Sit Through Mariel Rerun," Monday, February 23, 1981:13A.

829. Buchanan, Edna. "Latin Run Most Risk of Murder," Monday, February 15, 1982:1B.

830. Buchanan, Edna and Liz Balmaseda. "Mariel Cubans Melt Into S. Florida," Sunday, April 22, 1990:3A, 14A.

831. "Camp Personnel Deny Report of 20,000 Gay Refugees," Tuesday, July 8, 1980:1A.

832. "Captain Mariel Boatlift Beat U.S. Govt. $18,000 Fine," Wednesday, May 6, 1987: 1B.

833. Capuzzo, Michael. "Refugees Fill Ranks of Jobless," Saturday, December 20, 1980:1A.

834. Chardy, Alfonso. "Costa Rica Helps Take Up Where the Boatlift Left Off," Friday, March 20, 1981:32A.

835. _____. "Mariel Pact Advances, U.S. Says," Thursday, August 30, 1984:1A.

836. _____. "Rodino Bill is Attacked as Aid to Mariel Criminals," Saturday, May 19, 1984:14A.

837. _____. "U.S., Cuba Edge Toward Refugee Deal," Saturday, December 1, 1984:1A.

838. _____. "U.S., Cuba Fail to Reach Accord," Sunday, July

15, 1984:1A.

839. ____. "U.S. May Give Some Ground on Mariel Talks," Thursday, July 26, 1984:1A.

840. ____. "U.S. Shows No Interest in Talks Beyond Mariel," Saturday, July 28, 1984:14A.

841. ____. "Washington, Havana Plan A Second Round of Talks on Refugees," Saturday, July 21, 1984:15A.

842. "CIA: Castro Uso Exodo Para Refrenar Descontento," Sunday, June 2, 1980:4A.

843. Clary, Mike and Fabiola Santiago. "Status Symbol of Cuban Prisons Turns Into Brand of Infamy Here," Friday, July 23, 1982:3B.

844. ____. "The Baddest on the Block," Friday, July 23, 1982:1B.

845. "Cuban Austerity Could Spur Immigrant Flow, Experts Say," Tuesday, June 6, 1987:6A.

846. "Cuban-Immigration Deal Could Serve U.S. Interest," Saturday, January 17, 1981:6A.

847. "Cuban Multitudes March in "Carnival" for Castro," Sunday, May 18, 1980:24A.

848. "Cuban Spies Among Refugees, FBI Says," Thursday, May 8, 1980:1A.

849. "Desperately Seeking Any Way Out of Cuba," Wednesday, June 17, 1987:21A.

850. Díaz, Guarioné M. "La Cambiante Communidad Cubana," Sunday, August 16, 1981:9A.

851. "Dr. Miguel Fernández Reunited With Wife, Son After Seven Years," Friday, June 12, 1987:7A.

852. Ducassi, Jay. "Refugees Granted Extension on Status," Wednesday, July 15, 1981:22A.

853. ____. "Tapes Show Police Decision in Exile Riot," Tuesday, February 9, 1982:1B.

854. ____. "Two Visiting Exiles Detained in Cuba," Friday February 12, 1982:1A.

855. ____. "U.S. Skeleton Crew Presses Boatlift Cases," Sunday, January 17, 1982:2B.

856. Eady, Brenda. "Police Try to Understand Refugees' World," Monday February 15, 1982:2B.

857. "Elsa is Legal, At Least For Now," Sunday, May 10, 1987:5B.

858. "Exiles May Lose Political Status," Wednesday, April 30, 1980:4A.

859. Fabricio, Roberto, "Federal Policy on Immigration is Disturbing," Saturday, May 12, 1984:1B.

860. ____. "His Warnings Were Unheeded Until Too Late," Saturday, December 6, 1980:1B.

861. ____. "Old-Line Group Takes Notice of Mariel Factor," Saturday, August 25, 1984:1B.

862. "Fidel Calls Off Crisis For Carter," Wednesday, September 17, 1980:1A.

863. Fielder, Tom. "Refugee Proposal Favors Kin," Friday, February 27, 1981:1A.

864. Fielder, Tom and Guy Gugliotta. "How Resettlement Has Become a Mess," Saturday, June 1, 1984:1A.

865. Fielder, Tom and Richard Zaldivar. "U.S. May End Cuban Aid Program," Tuesday, March 17, 1981:1A.

866. "For the Mariel Misfits, Guantánamo Perfect," Friday, July 10, 1981:6A.

867. "Four On Tug Ask For Asylum," Tuesday, May 27, 1980:8A.

868. García, María C. "A Refugee's Reflections," Wednesday, April 21, 1982:1D.

869. Golden, Jeff. "Cuban's Deportation Came As Surprise to Shocked Reagan Aides," Saturday, January 23, 1982:1A.

870. ——. "Schools Hit By White Flight," Sunday, January 10, 1982:7B.

871. Grimm, Fred. "After Years of Arguments, A Quiet Departure," Friday, February 22, 1985:12A.

872. ——. "Judge Orders Parole for 34 Cubans," Thursday, January 17, 1985:1A.

873. ____. "The Mariel 23: From Horse Thieves to Murderers," Friday, February 22, 1985:12A.

874. Gyllenhaal, Anders and R.A. Zaldivar. "3,000 March in Little Havana," Sunday, January 17, 1982:1A.

875. Hampton, Jim. "Caged Logic on Cuban Prisoners," October 19, 1987:A12.

876. Harrison, Carlos. "Mariel Refugees Feel Isolated, Study Says," Tuesday, January 19, 1987:1A.

877. "Immigration: A Failure," Friday, July 27, 1984:18A.

878. "Immigration Reform," Tuesday, May 8, 1984:20A.

879. "INS Will Screen Mariels for Release," Saturday, June 6, 1987:21A.

880. "It's Up to the President to Curb Foreign Felons," Monday, December 7, 1981:6A.

881. Klement, Alice. "Two Priests Convicted for Roles at Mariels," Saturday, November 21, 1981:1A.

882. Kranish, M. "City Denies Sign up Aims at Cubans," September 22, 1983:: 46, E10.

883. ——. "U.S. Mariel Inmates Not Beach Bound," September 26, 1983: 46, E9.

884. McAden, Fitz and Joan Fleishman. "U.S. Gropes for Answers of Hijacks," Thursday, August 28, 1980:1A.

885. McCartney, James. "U.S. Ready to Lower Boom on Economic Life of Cuba," Thursday, February 11, 1982:1A.

886. McMullan, J. "The Other Side of Mariel," November 22, 1981:2E.

887. "Major Amendments Still Pending in Debate on Immigration Reform,"Sunday, June 17, 1984:18A.

888. "Mariel Offers Many Lessons," Tuesday, April 1, 1981:6A.

889. "Mariel Screenings," Monday, June 15, 1987:14A.

890. Martínez, G. "Filming of 'Scarface' Harms Cuban Image," August 28, 1982:18A.

891. _____. "Mariel Misfits Excluded from the Melting Pot," April 22, 1982: 19:E13.

892. _____. "U.S. Welfare Letter 'Offers' Refugees Chance to Relocate," May 4, 1982:1A, 11A.

893. _____. "Asylum is Still Just a Dream," Sunday, April 5, 1981:1A.

894. _____. "Boatlift's Legacy," Thursday, April 22, 1982:1A.

895. _____. "Children of Mariel Are Political Pawns," Thursday, March 4, 1982:33A.

896. _____. "Cuban Miamians Prone to Highlight How They Contrast With Marielitos," Tuesday, May 26, 1981:7A.

897. _____. "Deportation Lesson: Times Have Changed," Sunday, January 17, 1982:20A.

898. _____. "Forgotten in the Perú Embassy: Five Years After the Havana Incident Ignited Mariel," Friday, April 5, 1985:19A.

899. _____. "INS Defends Its Decision on Stowaway,"

Wednesday, January 20, 1982: 18A.

900. _____. "INS Makes Exceptions for Cubans," Tuesday, February 9, 1982:1A.

901. _____. "Mariel Criminals: Image, Reality," Friday, March 26, 1982:27A.

902. _____. "Mariel Refugees: A City Within a City," Sunday, December 14, 1980:1A.

903. _____. "Miami: It's Where the Migration Ends," Thursday, April 22, 1982:18A.

904. _____. "Reality of the Hispanic Dropout," Friday, January 27, 1984:25A.

905. _____. "Task-Force Proposal Would Allow Some Refugee to Become Citizens," Saturday, June 13, 1981:1A.

906. _____. "U.S.-Cuban Talks Collapse With No Accord On Refugees," Saturday, January 17, 1981:1A.

907. _____. "U.S. Might Admit More Cubans If Castro Takes Criminals Back," Thursday, January 15, 1981:1A.

908. Martinez, Guillermo and Fred Grimm. "Costa Rica Maneuvers for Exiles," Monday, April 21, 1980:1A.

909. Martínez, Guillermo and Robert Rivas. "Ragtag Flotilla Ferries Exiles," Thursday April 24,1980:1A.

910. Martínez, Guillermo and Helga Silva. "Marielitos Are Outraged Over Proposal, Others Are Thrilled to Receive Amnesty," Friday, July 31, 1981:14A.

911. Mártinez, Guillermo and Frederic Tasker. "Exiles Defy Warning on Boatlift," Friday, April 25, 1980:5A.

912. Melton, Eston. "Panel: Florida Due $146 Million for Refugees," Monday, January 25, 1982:1B.

913. "Mini-Rallies Jeer Cubans Wanting to Join Exodus," Friday, May 23, 1980:28A.

914. Montalbano, William D. "Baffled Stowaway: What Happened to Me?" Thursday, January 21, 1982:1A.

915. "Navy Ordered to Help Move Refugee Flotilla," Thursday, May 1, 1980:1A.

916. Nesbit, Jeff. "INS Turning the Tide on Backlog of Applications for Political Asylum," Sunday, April 1, 1984:19A.

817. "New Cuban Exodus Possible?" Monday, October 5, 1981:2A.

918. "1980 Mariel Brought Estimated 125,000 Cubans," Sunday, June 7, 1987:2B.

919. "1980 Mariel, 80,000 Settled in Date," Sunday, June 7, 1987:2B.

920. Oppenheimer, Andrés. "Mariel Made Area's Latins More Latin, Survey Found," Friday, April 29, 1983:1C.

921. "Parte de Miami Grupo a Cargo de Refugiados," Tuesday, August 8, 1980:1A.

922. "Reagan Must Not Ignore New Caribbean Entrants," Saturday, March 21, 1981:6A.

923. "Reagan Policy on Aliens Is Doubly Disappointing," Sunday, August 2, 1981:2E.

924. "Refugees Hold the Key to U.S.-Cuban Relations," Friday, May 1, 1981:6A.

925. Retter, Daniel. "Undocumented Alien Solution: A 90 Day Registration Grace," Monday, March 5, 1984:19A.

926. Rimer, Sara. "Refugee Odyssey," Friday, April 25, 1980:20A.

927. Rimer, Sara and David Hume. "Miamians Coping as Exiles Surge In," Monday, April 28, 1980:16A.

928. Rivas, Roberto and Janet Fix. "Fumes Kill Refugee Girl Abroad Boat," Saturday, August 30, 1980:18A.

929. Rivas, Roberto and David Hume. "Cubans Land Seasick, But Thrilled," Tuesday, April 22, 1980:1A.

930. Rose, Bill. "Atlanta Hispanics Working Way into Mainstream of Life in U.S." Sunday, May 2, 1982:16A.

931. _____. "Cubans in Atlanta Fear Refugees Will Ruin Image," Sunday, May 2, 1982:16A.

932. Rose, Willard P. "Some Refugees Are Imprisoned Without Crimes," Sunday, December 21, 1980:1A.

933. _____. "The Roybol Bill," Wednesday, February 8, 1984:18A.

934. Santiago, Fabiola. "Cuban Refugees Continue Lima Protest Camp," Friday, October 12, 1984:5A.

935. _____. "Cubans, Evicted From Lima Park, Stage Sit in Protest at U.N. Office," Friday, September 17, 1984:4A.

936. _____. "Don't Repeat Cuban's Deed, Petitions Say," Friday, February 22, 1985:11A.

937. _____. "Has Cuba's Crime Fallen Since Mariel?" Friday, December 25, 1981:9A.

938. _____. "Illegal Cuban Immigration on the Rise," Sunday, May 13, 1984:5B.

939. ____. "Like It or Not, Mariel Was a One Way Trip," Friday, April 23, 1982:18A.

940. ____. "Mariel Refugees: Free But in Legal Limbo," Sunday, September 25, 1983:26A.

941. ____. "Panamá is Dead End to Cubans," Sunday, April 1, 1984:29A.

942. ____. "Panamá Ring Smuggling Cubans to U.S.," Sunday, April 1, 1984:29A.

943. ____. "Plazo Final a 'Plantados' de Lima," Saturday, September 15, 1984:1A.

944. ____. "Report: East Little Havana A Slum in the Making," Wednesday, February 9, 1983:1D.

945. ____. "Tales of 3 Stowaways Are All Different," Saturday, January 30, 1982:1A.

946. ____. "Transatlantic Odyseey Ends; Cuban Refugees in Panama," Sunday, March 25, 1984:2A.

947. ____. "27 Refugees Share Mom in Miami," Monday, April 28, 1980:1A.

948. Santiago, Fabiola and Svdney P. Freedberg. "Influx Will Hasten Dade's Latinization," Monday, December 2, 1984:1A.

949. Santiago, Fabiola and Voboril, M. "Expected Cuban Influx Triggers Old Fear," December 4, 1984: 89:F10.

950. "Se Asila Entrenador de Natación en Puerto Rico," Saturday, May 30, 1980:2.

951. "Send Back Criminals," Monday, April 26, 1982:20A.

952. Shapiro, Margaret. "Hispanics Diversity Delays OK of Immigration Bill," Monday, March 19, 1984: 2A.

953. Shaw, Robert D., Jr. "Controversy Still Swirls Around Immigration Reform," Sunday, September 25, 1983:26A.

954. ____. "Distasteful Immigration Bills Still Drafting Stage," Monday, September 14, 1981:10A.

955. ____. "The New Policy: Who Can Stay, Who Can't," Friday, July 31, 1981:14A.

956. ____. "U.S. Will Turn Back Haitians: Refugee Proposals Outlines," Friday, July 31, 1981:1A.

957. ____. "Shockwaves of Mariel Sealift Continue to Rock Floridians," Wednesday, December 24, 1980:6A.

958. Silva, Helga. "Crime Fighers Focus On Mariel Elements," December 13, 1981:2C, 10C.

959. ____. "Criminals From Cuba Are Targets," Sunday,

December 10, 1981:1C.

960. ____. "Cuban Sent Home; Move is a First," Saturday, January 16, 1982:1A.

961. ____. "Hispanic Officials Change Face of City Governments," Sunday, May 18, 1984:1C.

962. ____. "Mariel Refugees Plan Crime Fighting Group," April 6, 1982:3B.

963. ____. "Refugee Aid Cut in Half in Congress," April 30, 1982: 19:F2.

964. ____. "Trends in Recent Months Suggest Worst of Crime Wave May Be Over," Friday, April 23, 1982:1A.

965. "Schools Believe 'White Flight' is Over," Thursday, November 10, 1983:1B.

966. "Some Refugees Suffer Psychological Problems," Thursday, May 1, 1980:16A.

967. "Statistics Given on Refugees," Wednesday, April 30, 1980:4A.

968. Stein, George and Guillermo Martínez. "Little Havana Attacked by Boatlift Criminals," Monday, September 8, 1980:1A.

969. Stasser, Fred. "Mariel Refugees Sue to Seek Same Status as Other Exiles," Friday, April 6, 1984:11C.

970. "Survey: Outlaw Hiring of Illegal Aliens," Sunday, November 13, 1983:10A.

971. Tasker, Frederic. "Anglo Flight is a Two Way Street," Sunday, November 16, 1980:1B.

972. ____. "Dade Gets Younger, More Mixed," Sunday, January 17, 1982:6B.

973. ____. "Dade Shows Melting Pot's A Myth," Thursday, January 14, 1982:1C.

974. ____. "Refugees Have Revised Census Data," Sunday, January 31, 1982:1B.

975. ____. "Refugees Influx Badly Outdates '80 Census Data," Sunday, January 31, 1982:1B.

976. Tasker, Frederic and Guillermo Martínez. "Castro's OK of Small Boat Exodus Creates Split for Miami Cubans," Wednesday, April 23, 1980:4A.

977. Tasker, Frederic and Helga Silva. "Latin Centers Spread, Transforming County," Sunday, February 14, 1982:1B.

978. Tasker, Frederic and Dan Williams. "100 Have Record,"

Wednesday, April 30, 1980:1B.

979. Taylor, Paul. "Illegal Aliens Cross Border to Live on Fringes of U.S. Middle Class," Sunday, June 17, 1984:18A.

980. "31 Cuban Prisoners Transferred to Secure Area After 8 Escape," Monday, August 20, 1984:6A.

981. "Three Cases of Leprosy," Saturday, May 17, 1980:1C.

982. "20,000 Gay Refugees Await Sponsor," Saturday, June 7, 1980:1A.

983. "U.S. May Legalize Refugees," Sunday, February 12, 1983:1A.

984. "U.S. Not Expecting Another Mariel," Saturday, June 13, 1987:6A.

985. "U.S. Open Arms to Cuban Exodus," Tuesday, May 6, 1980:1A.

986. Voboril, M. and Chardy, A. "Judge's Ban May Swap of Jailed Cubans for New Immigrants," December 12: 89:G4.

987. Vooril, Mary. "Indictments In Boatlift Thrown Out," Saturday, December 20, 1980:1A.

988. Wadler, Joyce. "Violent Mariel Refugees Plague New York Too," Sunday, December 13, 1981:1A.

989. "Wake From Mariel's Boats Still Washes South Florida," Sunday April 19, 1981:16A.

990. Walsh, Bryan O. "Immigration Policy: Drift in Dire Straits," Tuesday, May 10, 1983:15A.

991. _____. "Mariel, Crime and Scapegoats," Monday, December 29, 1980:6A.

992. "Washington Must Heed 'Marielito Murder Rate," Thursday, June 4, 1981:6A.

993. Williams, Dan. "Cuba Team Stalks Anti-Communist, Miami Police Say," Saturday, November 15, 1980:1A.

994. _____. "Processing Goes Orderly, But Housing Woes Near," Monday, April 28, 1980:1A.

995. Ynclan, Nery. "Celebrated Stowaway is Taken to Krome," Tuesday, January 2, 1982:1C.

996. _____. "Cubans Have a New Home, Old Problem," Saturday, February 6, 1982:12A.

997. _____. "Permanent Residency Seen Possible in '84 for Cubans, Haitians," Saturday, April 14, 1984:1A.

998. _____. "Stowaway on Freighter Sent to Krome," Thursday, January 14, 1982:2C.

999. Ynclan, Nery and Barbara Gutierrez. "Local Views Mixed on Return," Friday, February 22, 1985:13A.

1000. Zaldivar, R.A. "Black-Cuban Relations: Miami's Ethnic Puzzle," Sunday, March 25, 1984:1E.

1001. ____. "Deportation Probe By Hispanics," Tuesday, January 19, 1982:1A.

1002. ____. "Exile Communists Each See Alien Bill Differently," Sunday, June 17, 1984:22A.

1003. ____. "Top Justice OKs Ouster of Cubans," Saturday, February 2, 1985:1A.

1004. Zaldivar, R.A. and Fredd Grimm, "23 Mariel Inmates Sent Back," Friday, February 22, 1985:1A.

New York Times

1005. "Base in Puerto Rico to House Cubans and Haitians," Wednesday, September 24, 1980:20A.

1006. Battaile, Janet. "Cuban Exiles' Boat Pick Up 40 Refugees," Tuesday, April 21, 1980:7A.

1007. "Boatlift Creates Bizarre Twists, Some Humourous, Some Tragic," Tuesday, May 20, 1980:10B.

1008. Burkholz, Herbert. "The Latinization of Miami," Sunday, September 21, 1980:45F.

1009. "Businesses in Miami Suffer From Cuban Sealift Expense," Tuesday, July 8, 1980:12A.

1010. "Church is Seeking Sponsors for Homosexual Refugees," Monday, July 21, 1980:8A.

1011. Clymer, Adam. "Poll Links Economic Slide and Social Antagonism," Friday, June 27, 1980:1A.

1012. Crewdson, John M. "Airlift of Cubans in Key West Begins," Sunday, May 4, 1980:1A.

1013. ____. "Cubans Arrive in Key West; U.S. to Penalize the Flotilla," Thursday, April 24, 1980:1A.

1014. Crossette, Barbara. "U.S., Linking Cuba to Violence, Blocks Tourist and Business Trips," Tuesday, April 20, 1982:1A.

1015. "Cuba Bars Refugee Flights to Costa Rica Staging Area," Tuesday, April 19, 1980:6A.

1016. "Cuba Offers Talks on Return of Undesirables," Tuesday, June 26, 1983:8A.

1017. "Cuba Rejects Refugees' Return," Saturday, January 17, 1981:8A.

1018. "Cuban Offenders Get a Reprieve," Sunday, February 1, 1981:2E.

1019. "Cuban Refugee Unit Closing in Miami After Two Decades," Tuesday, September 8, 1981:18A.

1020. "Cuban Refugees Arrive at Center in Wisconsin," Monday, May 26, 1980:11A.

1021. "Cuban Refugees Continue to Slip Through Blockade," Tuesday, August 26, 1980:14A.

1022. "Cuban Refugees Hijack a Jetliner for Trip from Florida to Havana," Thursday, August 14, 1980:16A.

1023. "Cuban Refugees Scuffle With Guards in Florida," Sunday, May 25, 1980:30A.

1024. "Cubans Protests 3 Week Detention, Fight Police at Tent City in Florida," Monday, May 26, 1980:11A.

1025. "Cubans' Rescue Flotilla is Coming to a Standstill," Sunday, June 8, 1980:11A.

1026. "Cubans Riot at Camp in Arkansas; Police, Refugees and Civilian Hurt," Monday, June 2, 1980:1A.

1027. "Cubans Who Left Plane in Miami Won't Be Given Political Asylum," Thursday, April 2, 1981:19A.

1028. "Dejected Refugees Fill Miami Health Centers," Sunday, December 13, 1981:82A.

1029. "Detainees Fingerprinted," Sunday, November 13, 1983:73A.

1030. DeWitt, Karen. "First Cuban Refugees Arrive in Pennsylvania," Monday, May 19, 1980:9B.

1031. _____. "Jailing of Cuban Refugees Assailed as Unjust Process," Saturday, September 27, 1980:6A.

1032. "Dozens Hurt in Series of Protest by Cubans in Pennsylvania Camp," Wednesday, August 6, 1980:10A.

1033. Dunn, Marvin. "Miami's Explosion Isn't Miami Alone," Tuesday, May 20, 1980:19A.

1034. "8 People, 4 Companies Indicted in Cuba Sealift," Friday, February 26, 1982:14A.

1035. "Fairness of Case Reviews for Cubans is Challenged," January 3, 1988:A1.

1036. "First Refugees From Other Sites Start Arriving at Arkansas Camp," September 26, 1980:12A.

1037. "535 Refugees From Cuba Bound for Montana Base," December 19, 1981:10A.

1038. "Florida to Sue U.S. in Refugee Dispute," Saturday July 11, 1981:6A.

1039. "Florida Using U.S. Funds to Assist Refugees," Sunday June 6, 1982:22A.

1040. "Flow of Illegal Aliens Cut in Half in South Florida," Friday, February 20, 1987:1A.

1041. Gwertzman, Bernard. "U.S. Bids Cuba Take Several Thousand of Its Exiles Back," Thursday May 26, 1983:1A.

1042. "Havana Removes Guard From Peruvian Embassy," Saturday April 15, 1980:2A.

1043. "Healthy Cross Section of Emigres," Friday May 16, 1980:4A.

1044. Hoeffel, Paul Heath. "Fort Chafee's Unwanted Cubans," December 21, 1980:30-34.

1045. Jaynes, Gregory. "Fort Smith Has a Bad Morning After," Friday February 12, 1982:16A.

1046. "Jet Carrying 223 Forced to Cuba: Third in a Week," Friday August 15, 1980:12A.

1047. "Jet Hijacker is Identified as 1980 Cuban Refugee," Thursday February 4, 1982:16A.

1048. "Judge Orders Hearings for Jailed Cubans," Friday July 8, 1983:6A.

1049. "Judge Tells U.S. to Free 108 Cubans From Prison," Thursday, November 25, 1982:18A.

1050. Kneeland, Douglas E. "U.S. Admits Problems on Refugees; 14,000 Cubans Remain in Camps," Saturday August 30, 1980:1A.

1051. Lindsey, Robert. "U.S. is Finding That No One Wants to Accept Last Cuban Refugess," Sunday August 9, 1981:26A.

1052. McDowell, Edwin. "For Cuban Author, Liberty is Sweet," July 22, 1986:C15.

1053. "Marines Assist at Refugee Camps; 4,015 More Cubans Arrive by Boat," Thursday May 8, 1980:12A.

1054. "Miami Refugee Tent City Being Dismantled," Tuesday September 30, 1980:16A.

1055. "Miami Warned to Clean Up Tent City Housing Refugees," Sunday August 31, 1980:18A.

1056. Montgomery, Paul L. "Anger Long in Rising Among Miami's Blacks," May 19, 1980:1A.

1057. ____. "For Cuban Refugees, Promise of U.S. Fades," April 19, 1981:1A.

1058. ____. "Year Later, 1,800 Cubans Wait in U.S. Jails," April 27, 1981:1A.

1059. "More Cubans Arriving at Base Than Expected," May 21, 1980:24A.

1060. "Most in Poll Concerned Over Influx of Cubans," May 18, 1980:32A.

1061. Narvaez, Alfonso A. "Cuban Refugee Arriving in Jersey," May 4, 1980:1A.

1062. ____. "Cubans Finding the Good Life is Elusive," Jun15, 1980:1NJ.

1063. O'Connor, John J. "TV: Cuban Odysey, Refugee Drama," May 27, 1981:27C.

1064. "120 Cubans Reach U.S. as Airlift From Havana Begins," November 20, 1980:18A.

1065. Onis, Juan de. "Peru Asks Latins' Aid on Cubans," April 10, 1980:3A.

1066. Pear, Robert. "Many Cuban Exiles Left in the Lurch," November 26, 1980:14A.

1067. ____. "President to Treat Cubans as Applicants for Asylum," May 21, 1980:24A.

1068. ____. "President Toughens Curbs on Ferrying of Cuban Refugees," May 15, 1980:1A.

1069. ____. "Report on Refugees Urges a Crackdown," April 28, 1981:1A.

1070. ____. "U.S. Asked to Give Refugee Aid to Localities Quickly," June 5, 1980:21A.

1071. ____. "U.S. to Let Refugees From Cuba and Haiti Remain for 6 Months," June 21, 1980:1A.

1072. "Poll Finds Dissatisfaction," May 29, 1980:13A.

1073. Pound, Edward T. "Haitian-Cuban Cost Put at $532 Million," February 6, 1981:9A.

1074. Rawls, Wendell, Jr. "Drug Smuggling Surges on Gulf Coast," December 1, 1980:16A.

1075. Roberts, Steven V. "Economic Woes Strain Feelings in U.S. Toward Refugees," Sunday October 19, 1980:40A.

1076. Rohter, Larry. "U.S. Pact to Return Inmates to Havana

Alarms Emigres," September 30, 1993:16A.

1077. Schmidt, William E. "Detaining Cubans Exacts Rising Toll," March 10, 1986:1.

1078. Schumacher, Edward. "Cuban-Americans Argue in Mariel," May 3, 1980:7A.

1079. ____. "Cuban Exodus Bringing Defeat and Frustrations," May 6, 1980:12A.

1080. ____. "For Kin, Painful Choices in Cuba," May 7, 1980:14A.

1081. ____. "Retarded People and Criminals Are Included in Cuban Exodus," May 11, 1980:1A.

1082. "Seven Years Later, Mariel Aliens Outraged Over Jail," May 18, 1987:11A.

1083. Sheppard, Nathaniel, Jr. "Economic Standing Reflect Attitudes on Cuban Refugees," June 30, 1980:16A.

1084. Smothers, Ronald. "Sentences of Frustrations for Variety of Offenses," November 30, 1987.

1085. Stevens, William K. "Arkansas Fort Receives First of Thousands of Cubans," May 10, 1980:11A.

1086. Stuart, Reginald. "Detained Cubans: Policy in Confusion," August 24, 1981:12A.

1087. ____. "Judge Ready to Free 322 Cubans; Calls Handling of Exiles Disgrace," August 18, 1981:1A.

1088. ____. "356 Cubans Ordered Freed; Deporting of Others Barred," August 20, 1981:18A.

1089. ____. "3 Years Later, Most Cubans of Boatlift Adjusting to U.S.," May 17, 1983:1A.

1090. Sulzberger, A.O., Jr. "Ferrying of Refugees From Cuba to Florida is Condemned by U.S.," April 24, 1980:15A.

1091. Taylor, Stuart, Jr. "Reagan's Move to Control Immigration," November 4, 1981:21a.

1092. "Tears in a Cuban Port Marked End of Refugee Sealift," September 28, 1980:21A.

1093. "Text of State Department Statement on a Refugee Policy," June 21, 1980:18A.

1094. "32,000 Refugees Lose Federal Aid in Florida," June 2, 1982:18A.

1095. Thomas, Jo. "Amid Tension of Exodus to U.S., Havana Confronts Vast Social Ills," June 8, 1980:1A.

1096. ____. "Behind Barred Doors in Havana, Would-be

Emigres Wait in Fear," May 2, 1980:1A.

1097. ____. "Crowd at Havana Embassy Grows, 10,000 Reported Seeking Asylum," April 7, 1980:1A.

1098. ____. "Cuba Trucking Food and Water to Throng at Peruvian Embassy," April 9, 1980:1A.

1099. ____. "Hundreds in Havana Clash at U.S. Office," Saturday May 3, 1980:1A.

1100. ____. "Refugees in Miami Are Straining the City's Ability to Help Them," June 29, 1980:1A.

1101. ____. "3 Wounded at Embassy in Havana in Huge Throng of Asylum Seekers," April 10, 1980:1A.

1102. ____. "Troops Are Ordered to Arkansas Camp After Refugees Riot," June 3, 1980:1A.

1103. ____. "2,000 Who Want to Leave Cuba Crowd Peru's Embassy in Havana," April 6, 1980:1A.

1104. Tolchin, Martin. "Senators Restore $572 Million In Aid For States in 1980," June 28, 1980:1A.

1105. Treaster, Joseph B. "Call of Distress Among Rescuers of Cuba Emigres," April 26, 1980:13A.

1106. ____. "Coast Guard Begins Seizing Vessels Carrying Refugees," May 15, 1980:12A.

1107. ____. "Coast Guard Vessels and Aircraft Deployed to Cut off Boats to Cuba," May 18, 1980:1A.

1108. ____. "Refugees Pour in; Second Processing Center Slated," May 2, 1980:14A.

1109. ____. "Tide of Refugees Swell as Vessels With 500 Docks," May 12, 1980:12B.

1110. "25 Cuban Homosexuals Welcomed in San Francisco," Sunday, July 27, 1980:19A.

1111. "200 Cubans Flee Arkansas Camp," May 27, 1980:6B.

1112. "230 Cuban Refugees Arrive in Costa Rica," April 17, 1980:11A.

1113. "Two Priests Convicted for Ferrying Cubans," November 21, 1981:8A.

1114. "U.S. Deports First Cuban Since Castro Took Over," January 16, 1982:7A.

1115. "U.S. Fines Priests $1,000 for 1980 Boatlift," January 26, 1982:10A.

1116. Vidal, David. "Some Cubans Had `Wrong Idea' of U.S.," August 19, 1980:12A.

1117. Weinraub, Bernard. "Towns in Florida's Panhandle Wary Over Influx of Cuban Refugees," May 3, 1980:6A.

1118. Weisman, Steven R. "Havana Government Unilaterally Cuts Off Refugee Boat Exodus," September 27, 1980:1A.

1119. _____. "President Says U.S. Offers 'Open Arms' to Cuban Refugees," May 6, 1980:1A.

Washington Post

1120. Anderson, Jack. "Cuban Children," September 29, 1980:11B.

1121. _____. "GSA Pocketbook Showers Goodies on Cuban Exiles," July 16, 1981:7B.

1122. Babcock, Charles R. "FBI Discovering Some 'Undesirables' Among Flood of Refugees From Cuba," April 29, 1980:4A.

1123. _____. "Resettling of Cuban Refugees is Proceeding at a Slow Rate," February 10, 1981:7A.

1124. _____. "U.S. is Preparing Md., Pa., Bases as Refugee Centers," May 12, 1980:1A.

1125. _____. "U.S. to Create Special Status for Caribbean Refugees," Friday June 20, 1980:1A.

1126. Bazan, Joaquin, Reverend. "The Cubans," October 1, 1980:28A.

1127. "Bill For Cubans Abroad: Refugees in 3rd Countries," March 24, 1987:5A.

1128. "Boat People: The Cubans...?" January 8, 1983:22A.

1129. Brown, Warren. "Cuban Boatlift Drew Thousands of Homosexuals," July 7, 1980:1A.

1130. _____. "Red Tape Can Entangle Even Cubans Who Pass the Tests," June 5, 1980:7A.

1131. _____. "U.S. to Ask Hemisphere to Share Cuban Refugees," July 22, 1980:11A.

1132. Charles, Serge E. "Refugees From Poverty," May 31, 1980:14A.

1133. Cody, Edward. "Florida's Havana: With Latin's in Miami, The Melting Pot Melts," May 14, 1983:1A.

1134. "Cuban Sealift Comes to a Halt," June 15, 1980:26A.

1135. Dickey, Christopher. "Cuban Exodus Tarnishes Castro's Image," June 7, 1980:19A.

1136. ____. "22 Nations Offer Limited Aid to Cuban Exodus," May 9, 1980:33A.

1137. Diehl, Jackson. "Cuban Refugees Stranded in Lima Dream of Refuge in U.S.," October 29, 1982:25A.

1138. DuBuclet, Linda. "Cuban Refugee, Cat Lived in Hole, Hut at the National Zoo," March 13, 1984:1A.

1139. "80 Cuban Refugees Ending Up in Florida as Victims of Homicide," June 1, 1981:12A.

1140. Evan, John K. "A Welcome For Setbacks," May 24, 1980:24A.

1141. Fix, Janet and Anders Gyllenhaal. "Boats Forced to Bring Convicts and Mental Patients Reaches Florida," May 12, 1980:14A.

1142. Harris, Art. "Jailed Mariel Refugees Languish in Limbo Between Cuba and U.S.," May 26, 1983:2A.

1143. ____. "Judge Rules for Rights of Cubans," July 8, 1984:1A.

1144. Hornblower, Margot. "Aspin Says CIA Foretold of Massive Influx of Cubans," June 2, 1980:6A.

1145. ____. "U.S. Moves 500 Cubans to Florida Holding Center," May 4, 1980:24A.

1146. Johnson, Janis. "Anti-Latin Rage: A War of Words Wage in Miami," Saturday September 30, 1980:1A.

1147. ____. "Miami Homicides at Record-killing Pace," November 19, 1980:15A.

1148. Joyce, Maureen. "Cutbacks Limit Aid to Refugees," June 30, 1982:Md1.

1149. "Justice Asks Courts to Block Release of Cubans," August 31, 1983:4A.

1150. Kastenmeir, Robert W. "Mariel Cubans Deserve Due Process Too," March 24, 12A.

1151. Lemann, Nicolas. "Refugees Hope They'll be Prosperous as Well as Free," May 9, 1980:34A.

1152. "Majority of Cuban Immigrants Fled After Castro Take-Over," August 16, 1982:10A.

1153. Murphy, Caryle. "105,000 Persons Asking U.S. For Asylum Set Record, Clog Bureaucratic Machinery," June 28, 1982:1A.

1154. Nunes, Donnel. "Cuban Children Arriving Parentless," June 1, 1980:1A.

1155. "Outrageous View of New Immigration Laws," May 25, 1986:14A.

1156. Raspberry, William. "Their Tired, Their Poor-Our Jobs," July 4, 1980:15A.

1157. Russakoff, Dale and Stephanie Mansfield. "U.S. Drops Plan to Use Md. Base in Processing Cuban Refugees," May 14, 1980:1C.

1158. Schram, Martin and Charles R. Babcock. "Carter's Ad Lib Affected Policy," May 15, 1980:1A.

1159. Simons, Marlise. "Castro Says U.S. Must Accept Refugees," May 2, 1980:22A.

1160. ____. "Castro Skillfully Deflects Seeming Setback to His Own Political Advantage," May 1, 1980:38A.

1161. ____. "Costa Rica Offers Home for 10,000 Cuban Refugees," April 21, 1980:1A.

1162. ____. "Cuba Approves Refugee's Departure in Florida-Chartered Flotilla of Boats," April 22, 1980:14A.

1163. ____. "Cuba Suddenly Permits Mass Emigration to U.S.," April 29, 1980:1A.

1164. ____. "For 750 Cuban Refugees, U.S. is a Tent City-Under the Expressway," September 22, 1980:5A.

1165 .____. "Somber Cuban Refugees Jam Shrimp Boat to Flee to U.S.," April 23, 1980:21A.

1166. Thornton, Mary. "Cubans Bound for Montana," December 19, 1981:14A.

1167. "U.S. Gives Cuba List of Boatlift Refugees Ineligible to Remain," May 26, 1983:30A.

1168. "U.S. May Move Remaining Exiles to Single Camp," July 10, 1980:11A.

1169. "U.S. Officials Warn Against Unauthorized Refugee Trips," April 23, 180:21A.

1170. Valente, Judith. "Clashing Waves of Cuban Refugees," September 20, 1981:1C.

1171. ____. "Cubans in D.C. Still on the Outside," April 13, 1982:19A.

1172. ____. "$1 Million Fund to Resettle Cubans Here Wasted, City Say," December 15, 1981:1A.

1173. ____. "U.S. Cutting off Funds to City Refugee

Programs," March 13, 1982:7B.

1174. Wadler, Joyce and Alexandra D. Korry. "For Refugees, The Ordeal Won't End," September 9, 1980:1A.

1175. Walsh, Edward. "2nd Center to Open," May 8, 1980:1A.

1176. Walsh, Edward and John M. Goshko. "Chaffee Troops Tripled; Faster Processing Set," June 3, 1980:1A.

Los Angeles Times

1177. "Andean Pact Meets on Cuban Refugees," April 10, 1980:5.

1178. Berholz, Richard. "Reagan Urges `Berlin Airlift' Rescue of Cubans," April 10, 1980:18.

1179. "Carter Says Illegal Cuban Boatlift Must Stop, Orders Prosecution," June 6, 1980:9.

1180. "Cuba Says All Seeking Exile Will Be Let Go," April 7, 1980:2.

1181. Curry, Bill. "Added Troops Help Calm Riot-Torn Refugee Camp," June 3, 1980:6.

1182. "Exile Identified by Fellow Cubans as Castro Guard," May 6, 1980:5.

1183. "5 Latin Nations to Take Cuban Refugees," April 11, 1980:11.

1184. Irwin, Don. "Ours in a Country of Refugees, President Says," May 6, 1980:5.

1185. _____. "Study Outlining Possible Way to Deport Criminal Refugees Ordered by Carter," June 5, 1980:7.

1186. _____. "U.S. to Admit Up to 3,500 Cubans," April 15, 1980:6.

1187. "Key West Merchants See `Horrendous Headlines' on Exiles as Tourism Threat," May 15, 1980:13.

1188. "Many Former Convicts Reported on Board Latest U.S. Vessel to Return From Cuba," June 8, 1980:4.

1189. May, Lee. "L.A. Complains of Refugee Cost," June 4, 1980:15.

1190. _____. "Officials Work to Weed Out Wayward Refugees," May 14, 1980:4.

1191. _____. "Only 2 Nations to Take Cubans," May 31, 1980:1.

1192. _____. "Refugee Sea-Airlift Offered," May 15, 1980:1.

1193. Nelson, Jack. "Refugee Could Exceed 100,000, Carter Aide Says," May 21, 1980:17.

1194. "1,300 Cubans Seeking Asylum Flee to Embassy," April 6, 1980:1.

1195. Ostrow, Ronald J. "1,395 Cuban Refugees in U.S. Prisons for Serious Crimes Committed in Cuba," July 1, 1980:4.

1196. Prugh, Jeff. "A 20 Year Wait Ends in Smiles, Tears," May 2, 1980:10.

1197. _____. "Cuba Scorns Carter's Move to Halt Boatlift," May 16, 1980:1.

1198. _____. "Hope, Sound of See Gees Bring Cubans to U.S.," May 4, 1980:1.

1199. _____. "Refugees Reportedly Include Many Criminals," April 30, 1980:1.

1200. _____. "Refugees Tell of Scramble for Food," April 26, 1980:2.

1201. _____. "Surge of Cuban Refugees Strains Reception Facilities," May 5, 1980:1.

1202. Rempel, William C. "Boatlift of Cubans Grow in Face of Warning by U.S.," April 25, 1980:1.

1203. _____. "Health of Cuban Refugees Deteriorating, Doctors Say," May 1, 1980:1.

1204. _____. "20 Small Boats Discovered Adrift in Florida Straits," April 29, 1980:1.

1205. Rempel, William C. and Ronald J. Ostrow. "Influx Hits 3,500; Use of Small Craft Decried," April 30. 1980:1.

1206. "Renewal of Boatlift Called a Possibility," July 21, 1980:4.

1207. Shannon, Don. "Big Havana Crowd Denounces Refugees," April 20, 1980:18.

1208. _____. "Boat Owners 'Playing Into Hands of Cuba Authorities' on Refugees, U.S. Charges," April 24, 1980:4.

1209. _____. "Castro's Problems Mount-Cuba Called Under Siege," May 2, 1980:10.

1210. _____. "Costa Rica Offers Asylum to All 10,000 Cubans," April 21, 1980:1.

1211. _____. "Cuba Defectors Attacked, Seek Satety in U.S. Office," May 3, 1980:1.

1212. _____. "Cuban Harbor Full of Boats," May 11, 1980:24.

1213. _____. "Havana Mood Changes, But Some Emigrants Are Still Jeered," May 25, 1980:4.

1214. "Skipper, 66 Cuban-Americans Arrested as They Bring 100,000th Refugee to U.S.," May 25, 1980:14.

1215. Toth, Robert C. "Castro Suspected of Confrontation Ploy," May 14, 1980:4.

1216. _____. "U.S. Seeks Help Abroad for Refugees," May 8, 1980:1.

1217. Toth, Robert C. and Oswald Johnston. "Exodus Seen As Major Blow to Castro," April 20, 1980:1.

1218. Townsend, Dorothy and Jerry Belcher. "Last Stop on Way to New Life," May 10, 1980:1.

1219. "2 Cuban Exile Boats Land 40 Refugees in Florida," April 22, 1980:5.

1220. "2 Planeloads of Cuban Refugees Reach Costa Rica," April 17, 1980:1.

1221. Will, George F. "For 'Maximum Leader' Castro No Alibi," April 28, 1980:5.

Granma Weekly Review

1222. Alarcon Quesada, Ricardo. "Steel and Scum," May 25, 1980:5.

1223. "Antisocial Elements Continue Causing Distubances in Yankee Paradise," June 8, 1980:16.

1224. Arce, Luis Manuel. "The Danger Behind the Vile Campaign Against Cuba," April 20, 1980:6.

1225. "Biographical Data on Private Pedro Ortiz Cabrera, Guard at the Peruvian Embassy Who Was Killed on April 1," April 13, 1980:1.

1226. "Cuba's Position," April 13, 1980:1.

1227. Ferrer, Oscar. "An Anti-Cuban Plan Born of Failure," April 20, 1980:7.

1228. "Figures Speak for Themselves," April 20, 1980:6.

1229. Garcia, Julio. "The Beginning," June 15, 1980:2.

1230. "International Expression of Support for Cuba," April 20, 1980:4.

1231. Marrero, Juan. "Garbage Dump Started By

Imperialists," June 1, 1980:3.

1232. "News from Mariel," April 27, 1980:9.

1233. "News from the Peruvian Embassy," June 15, 1980:1.

1234. "The People Will Go Into Action," April 20, 1980:1.

1235. "Pinochet Wants to Take Some Lumpen Elements, But He Wants Them Hand Picked," April 20, 1980:5.

1236. Ramos, Rafael. "30 Wounded in Ft. Chafee in Clash Between Yankee Police and Anti-Social Elements," June 15, 1980:5.

1237. Rojas, Marta. "The Spirit Renewed in the Young Generation," April 27, 1980:9.

1238. Sosa, Manuel Robles. "Situation of Anti-Social Elements Taken in by Peruvian Government Looks Tense," May 4, 1980:10.

1239. "Statement by the Revolutionary Government of Cuba," April 13, 1980:1.

1240. Telleria, Evelio. "Biggest Mass Rally in Cuban History," May 11, 1980:10.

1241. ____. "Millions of Cubans Express Repudiation for U.S. Imperialism in March of the Fighting People," May 25, 1980:5.

1242. Valera, Orestes. "The Real Side of the Coin," April 20, 1980:5.

1243. "What's Carazo Up to Now?" May 18, 1980:3.

1244. "Yankee Bewilderment and Confusion," May 4, 1980:1

1245. "Yankee Embarrassment," May 18, 1980:4.

1246. "Yankee Legislator Advocates Return Tickets for Insubordinate Anti-Social Elements," June 14, 1980:2.

1247. "Yankee Provocation at the U.S. Interests Section," May 11, 1980:1.

Arkansas Democrat

1248. "Army Seeks to Quiet Concern About Chaffee," May 21, 1980: 103.

1249. Ault, Larry. "Ms. Rodham Defends Handling of Chaffee," June 4, 1980: B.

1250. Brewer, Steve. "Texas Center Awaits Cubans," June 8, 1980

1251. "Carter Dispatches Troops to Chaffee," June 3, 1980:

Front Page.

1252. "Carter to Speed Processing on Deportation For Cubans," June 5, 1980: 10 A, 11A.

1253. "Carter Wants Cubans Riffraff Out," June 7, 1980: Front Page.

1254. "Chaffee Nears Refugee Limit," May 18, 1980: 11A.

1255. "Chaffee Worker Owes Life to "amigos"," June 4, 1980: 15A.

1256. "Clinton Wants to 'Beef Up' Fort Chaffee Security," May 20, 1980.

1257. "Cuban Mob Denounces Mass Exodus," May 18, 1980: Front Page.

1258. "Dart of Blame for Chaffee Riot," June 8, 1980: 4E.

1259. Fellone, Franf. "Clinton Supports Shootings," June 7, 1980: Front Page.

1260. _____. "Gunshots Scatter Refugees," June 2, 1980.

1261. "Fort Chaffee Camp Quiet After Security Boosted," June 9, 1980.

1262. "Fort Chaffee at Capacity ; Refugee Flow to Stop For a Week," May 20, 1980.

1263. "Group Makes Plea For Understanding of Cuban Refugees," June 20, 1980: 8A.

1264. Howell, Cynthia. "Bumpers Questions Reasons For Transfer," January 25, 1982: Front Page.

1265. Oakley, Meredith. "Clark to Probe Military's Action at Fort," June 18, 1980.

1266. "Officials Charging Refugee 'Disaster'," May 20, 1980.

1267. "100,000th. Cuban Refugees Arrives," June 4, 1980: 8A.

1268. "Refugees Only Want Liberty, Revolt Leader Says," June 9, 1980: 9A.

1269. "Refugee Ship Sinks; 10 Dead," May 18, 1980: Front Page.

1270. Rothenberg, Mike. "Commander Confident of Controlling Chaffee," June 4, 1980: Front Page.

1271. _____. "Communication Major Problem," June 5, 1980: 10A.

1272. _____. "Cuban Father and Son Reunited at Chaffee After 20 Years," May 16, 1980: 17 A.

1273. _____. "This Cuban Refugee's Story Puts Him in a Class

By Himself," May 15, 1980.

1274. "Searchers Take Cubans Weapons, Wiskey," June 7, 1980.

1275. Speed, Kay. "Cubans Face Longer Stay in Prison," January 21, 1982: Front Page.

1276. Tucker, Tyler. "Fort 'Calm' After Security Increased," June 4, 1980: 16A.

1277. "Waiting Game Draws Protest From Refugees," June 17, 1980.

1278. Weisman, Dan. "Clinton to Ask Aid on Costs at Chaffee," June 17, 1980.

Arkansas Gazette

1279. Arnold, Michael. "Agreement to Transfer Cubans Will be Drafted," December 18, 1981:C5.

1280. _____. "Glasgow Again Under Review," December 12, 1981:C4.

1281. _____. "Group From Montana Tours Chaffee, Says It's Impressed by What it Sees," September 18, 1981:E12.

1282. _____. "Not All From Chaffee May Go To Montana," September 21, 1981:A1.

1283. _____. "Security Plans to be Changed at For Chaffee," April 26, 1981:D1.

1284. _____. "72 Cubans Resettled; 892 Still at Fort," June 30, 1981:A3.

1285. _____. "Social, Political Aftershocks Remain From Chaffee Riot," December 20, 1981:B2.

1286. _____. "Time to Decide Fate of Cubans, Officials Say," February 17, 1981:C14.

1287. Fair, Elizabeth. "Cubans Anger Sheriff," July 23, 1981:E14.

1288. Hamburger, Tom. "U.S. Considers 2 Refugee Sites," August 11, 1981:F4.

1289. _____. "White Says He Got Assurances Administration Working 'Agressively' to Relocate Refugees," August 31, 1981:F1.

1290. Hamburger, Tom and Michael Arnold. "Decision Made, Refugees Going to Montana, White Told," December 1, 1981:C6.

1291. "Montana Group Considering Plan for Refugee Camp,"

September 3, 1981:G13.

1292. "Refugee Center Wins Approval," September 14, 1981:G14.

1293. Watson, Peggy. "Officers Warned About Picking Up Cubans," May 24, 1980:E13.

1294. _____. "Screening of Refugees Reveals Fourth Have Questionable Past," May 18, 1980:E9.

1295. "Alexander Express Compassion For Cubans, Backs Castro's Ouster," May 17, 1980: 1A

1296. "Alexander Urges U.S. To Detain Refugees," May 13, 1980: 1A

1297. "All Boats Headed For Cuba Halted, Searched by U.S.," May 17, 1980: 3A

1298. "Anxieties Grow as Transfer Of Cubans to Chaffee Nears," September 14, 1980: 1A

1299. "Army Ordered To Keep Troops At Chaffee," September 5, 1980: 1A

1300. "Army to Begin Moving Troops From Chaffee," December 7, 1980: 4A

1301. "Army Wants Pullout Of Chaffee Troops; Affects Security Plan," September 5, 1980: 1A

1302. "Arraignment Planned For 6 Cuban Refugees," November 7, 1980: 14A

1303. "Arrests of Refugees Illegal, Clark Declares," September 26, 1980: 1A

1304. "Aspin Says Castro Planning Another Flood of Refugees," June 23, 1980: 7A

1305. "Assigned Guard Changes at Fort," December 14, 1980: 2A

1306. "Assault Trial of Cuban Moved to Hot Springs," December 17. 1980: 19A

1307. "Asylum Offered 10,000 Cubans," April 21, 1980: 2A

1308. "Barracks Burns At Chaffee," November 21, 1980: 3A

1309. "Better to Delay Security Plan Pact, Clark Tells Clinton," September 26, 1980: 2A

1310. "Bigger Influx Of Refugees Seen at Chaffee," May 12, 1980: 1A

1311. "Breakdown Limits Airlift of Cubans, 2 Flights Carry 186," October 3, 1980:6A

1312. "Bumpers Upset About Inquiry In Chaffee Riot," June

4, 1980: 1A

1313. "Carter Admits 3,500 Cubans As Refugess," April 15, 1980: 1A

1314. "Carter's Aide Apologizes, But Says Cubans Due Soon," August 6, 1980: 1A

1315. "Carter Offers 'Open Arms' To Thousands Fleeing Cuba," May 6, 1980: 2A

1316. "Carter Orders All Criminals Be Returned," June 8, 1980: 1A

1317. "Carter Promises to Consult Clinton," August 5, 1980: 1A

1318. "Carter Urged to Deputize Chaffee Troops," May 30, 1980: 2A

1319. "Case-by-case Review Of Refugees Studied," May 13, 1980: 1A

1320. "Castro 'Gave It to Us With Two Barrels,' Immigration Agent Says of Exodus," August 31, 1980: 24A

1321. "Castro Bans Refugee Flights To Costa Rica," April 19, 1980: 17A

1322. "Celebration Happens At Chaffee," December 1, 1980:10A

1323. "Chaffee-area Officials Discuss Cubans, Bid For Aid at Washington," August 21, 1980: 13A

1324. "Chaffee Authorities Will Change Tuberculosis Screening Procedure," October 15, 1980:

1325. "Chaffee Barracks Damaged by Fire; Refugee Arrested," September 16, 1980: p 1A

1326. "Chaffee Decision Wasn't Political, Carter Aide Says," October 10, 1980: 1A

1327. "Chaffee Force Up to Task, Clinton Advised," December 20, 1980, 5A

1328. "Chaffee Gets Last Planeload Of Refugees," October 10, 1980: 14A

1329. "Chaffee Policy Changed, Refugees Must Have Clearances to Leave," June 10, 1980: 1A

1330. "Chaffee Officials Expect Late Closing," November 15, 1980: 1A

1331. "Chaffee Speeds Processing, 558 Leave Fort," June 10, 1980: 11A

1332. "Chaffee To Process 466 Today," June 23, 1980: 8A

1333. "Chaffee Troops Ordered to Stay," September 6, 1980: 3A

1334. "Chaffee Troops Trimmed by 350 After Transfers," December 8, 1980: 3A

1335. "Claim Is Filed In Chaffee Riot," September 19, 1980: 6A

1336. "Clark Delays Suit on Status Of Refugees," October 15, 1980: 12A

1337. "Clark Says U.S. Should Expel Certain Cubans," September 13, 1980: 3A

1338. "Clark Tours Cuban Refugee Center," July 17, 1980: 7A

1339. "Clinton Approves Plans for Chaffee; Flights Start Today," September 25, 1980: 1A

1340. "Clinton Fears Trouble at Fort," June 13, 1980: 1A

1341. "Clinton Notes Reservations Remaining on Chaffee Plan," September 21, 1980: 9A

1342. "Clinton Offers Plan to Check Cuba Refugees," May 14, 1980: 2A

1343. "Clinton Plans Chaffee Talks," August 3, 1980: 1A

1344. "Clinton Postpones Refugee Transfer, Cites Reservations," September 11, 1980: 3A

1345. "Clinton Outlines His Interpretation Of Security Pact," September 30, 1980: 4A

1346. "Clinton Won't Accept Cuban Troublemakers," September 11, 1980:1A

1347. "Closing of 2 Refugee Camps Ordered by Health Officials," September 11, 1980: 3A

1348. "Crime Wave Blamed on Cuban Refugees, Illict Drug War,..."January 1, 1981

1349. "Criminals Included In Refugee Sealift; Facilities Strained," May 2, 1980: 21A

1350. "Cuba May Release 150,000 to U.S., Department Says," May 11, 1980: 1A

1351. "Cuba Refugees In U.S. Custody, Official Says," September 27, 1980: 1A

1352. "Cuba Rejects Call for Talks About Refugees," May 24, 1980: 2A

1353. "Cuba Spies Found Among Refugees, FBI Agent Reports," July 7, 1980: 3A

1354. "Cuba Turns Down Offer to Negotiate Refugee Return,"

August 23, 1980:1A

1355. "Cuban Crowd Labels Refugees 'Parasites'," April 20, 1980: 27A

1356. "Cuban, 18, Is Arrested In Stabbing," October 24, 1980: 5A

1357. "Cuban Exiles Assemble Flotilla to Carry Food, Medicine to Embassy," April 14, 1980: 4A

1358. "Cuban Exodus: Is Washington Missing the Boat?" May 11, 1980

1359. "Cuban Flow Eases; Agency Will Close Key West Offices," June 7, 1980: 1A

1360. "Cuban Refugee Enters Guilty Plea, Sentenced to Year in State Prison," September 19, 1980: 7A

1361. "Cuban Refugee Held in Slaying," September 16, 1980: 1A

1362. "Cuban Refugee Is Charged In Stabbing," November 25, 1980: 5A

1363. "Cuban Stabbed At Fort Chaffee," September 10, 1980: 13A

1364. "Cubans Assist At Flag Raising," November 12, 1980: 4A

1365. "Cubans at Chaffee Enjoy Traditional Holidays Fare," November 28, 1980: 3A

1366. "Cubans Begin Arriving From Pennsylvania Fort In Final Phase of Move," October 7, 1980: 9A

1367. "Cubans Flee Fort Chaffee; Some Captured," May 27, 1980: 6A

1368. "Cubans Forced Him to Overload Ship, Skipper Says; Toll Rises to 14, "May 19, 1980: 6A

1369. "Cubans Left at Chaffee Developing Mood of Resignation," November 21, 1980: 8A

1370. "Cubans Lukewarm to English Classes," October 12, 1980: 1A

1371. "Cubans Rush Gate During Protests By Kin, Residents," May 30, 1980: 2A

1372. "Cubans Saved In Stormy Seas," April 29, 1980: 1A

1373. "Cubans Seeking Visas Assaulted By Armed Agents," May 3, 1980: 3A

1374. "Cubans Swing Chairs At Chaffee Officer, Eight Injured in Fracas," October 9, 1980:4A

1375. "Cubans Swarm Peru Embassy," April 6, 1980: 1A
1376. "Cubans to Arrive By End of Week If Plan Approved," September 24, 1980: 1A
1377. "Cubans to Be Searched For Weapons, Moved Under Strict Security," September 25, 1980: 3A
1378. "Cultists Quit at Chaffee," August 5, 1980: 1A
1379. "Cultists Work, 'Witness' at Chaffee," July 23, 1980: 1A
1380. "Decision Due On FBI Report Of Chaffee Riot," August 9, 1980: 3A
1381. "Delay Cubans, Officials Ask," August 26, 1980: 1A
1382. "Demands by Clinton On Chaffee Security Had Been Met Earlier," September 12, 1980: 1A
1383. "Director Named At Fort Chaffee," November 1, 1980: 15a
1384. "Doctors Say Chaffee Neglecting Refugees; Mental Cases Alleged," September 17, 1980: 4A
1385. "Drug Arrest Made at Fort," June 17, 1980: 4A
1386. "85 Pct. Of Cubans Resettled; 15,000 'Hard Core' Left," September 6, 1980: 8A
1387. "Eglin Increases Security After Scuffle," May 26, 1980: 1A
1388. "11 Agents Are Sent To Chaffee," May 20, 1980: 2A
1389. "Emergency Declared In Florida; $10 Million In Aid Is Authorized," May 7, 1980: 1A
1390. "Exodus From Cuba," May 11, 1980: 4E
1391. "FBI Investigates Abuse Charges At Fort Chaffee," January 15, 1981
1392. "FBI Reportedly Upset by Chaffee Shortcuts in Processing Cubans," June 7, 1980: 1A
1393. "Federal Officials Respond To Objections by Clinton," September 17, 1980: 4A
1394. "First Flight Brings 128 Cuban Men For Fort Chaffee," May 10, 1980: 1A
1395. "First McCoy Refugees Reach Fort Chaffee," September 27, 1980: 1A
1396. "First Refugees Reach Center," May 4, 1980: 1A
1397. "5 Cubans, Officer Are Injured in Fire, Arson Suspected," October 30, 1980: 14A
1398. "5 Ex-prisoners in Cuba Face Deportation, Official Says," May 21, 1980: 3A

1399. "15 at Chaffee Held In Security Area," December 4, 1980: 8A

1400. "15 Members of Klan Hold Protest At Fort Smith Against Refugee," May 25, 1980: 1A

1401. "542 More Refugees Arrive at Chaffee as Consolidation Continues Smoothly," September 30, 1980: 4A

1402. "5,893 Cubans Still Remain At Chaffee," January 4, 1981: 4A

1403. "441 Soldiers To Leave Fort," June 21, 1980: 1A

1404. "Fort Chaffee Guards Suffering From Heat," July 2, 1980: 10A

1405. "Fort Chaffee Refugee Dies; Natural Causes Suspected," July 12, 1980: 7A

1406. "Fort Chaffee to House Refugees From Cuba," May 8, 1980: 1A

1407. "Fort Processes 3, 304 Refugees," June 19, 1980: 6A

1408. "Fort Security Improved, State Police To Stay, Clinton Says," June 7, 1980: 2A

1409. "42 Cubans Continue Food Strike," September 28, 1980: 1A

1410. "Four Cuban Refugees Ordered Deported, More Await Decision on Asylum in Florida," June 20, 1980, 15A

1411. "Four Refugees Sent to Chaffee After Tests," November 11, 1980: 3A

1412. "'Freedom Flotilla' Could End Soon," May 28, 1980: 3A

1413. "Gang Fights Threaten Chaffee Peace," November 19, 1980: 1A

1414. "Governor Visits Fort Chaffee, Says Difficulties Remain," June 17, 1980: 5A

1415. "Guards Halt Cuban Rush Toward Gate," May 30, 1980: 1A

1416. "Halfway House Near Fort Chaffee Aids Returned Refugees," August 3, 1980: 4A

1417. "Haiti, Cuban Refugees To Apply for Extension Of Time to Stay in U.S.," June 27, 1980: 21A

1418. "'Homecoming' Greets Latest Cubans," September 28, 1980: 1A

1419. "House Approves Measure To Pay Back Refugee Aid," June 20, 1980: 16A

1420. "Hundreds Freed After Threat," June 11, 1980: 1A

1421. "Hundreds More Flee Cuba; 25 Detained," May 1, 1980: 22A

1422. "Instructions on Force Vary at Cuban Centers," June 11, 1980: 2A

1423. "Lawmakers To Visit Refugees," May 14, 1980: 2A

1424. "Letter Satisfies Clark, Won't File Refugees Suit," October 25, 1980: 4A

1425. "Military Leaving 3 Chaffee Areas; Problems Feared," August 1, 1980: 1A

1426. "More Cuban Refugees Reach Florida; Victim Is Taken From Boat," May 12, 1980: 1A

1427. "More Detailed Response Needed On Security Proposal, Clinton Says," September 19, 1980: 6A

1428. "More Refugees Arrive; First Refugees Begin Dispersal to Sponsors," May 10, 1980: 3A

1429. "More Refugees Arrive; Officials Closing Facility," June 11, 1980: 2A

1430. "Mother, Son From Cuba Reunited at Fort Chaffee," December 10, 1980: 7A

1431. "NCCJ Asks Understanding For Law-abiding Refugees," June 20, 1980: 16A

1432. "The New Policy on Refugees," May 17, 1980: 12A

1433. "No 'Witnessing' Allowed at Fort," July 24, 1980: 1A

1434. "NW Arkansas Officials Visit Washington to Discuss Chaffee," August 20, 1980: 14A

1435. "Official Cites Difficulties In Relocating Refugees," November 7, 1980: 14A

1436. "Officials Blamed for Chaffee's Image," November 29, 1980: 1A

1437. "107 Cubans Fly To Costa Rica," April 25, 1980: 24A

1438. "115 Cubans Get Sponsors," October 23, 1980: 21A

1439. "157 Refugees To Leave Fort," June 25, 1980

1440. "120 Cuban Refugees Stranded at Mariel Are Airlifted to U.S.," November 20, 1980:13A

1441. "120 Leaving Chaffee; 4,000 Need Sponsors," January 27, 1981

1442. "$100 Million Is Voted By House to Resettle Cuba, Haiti Refugees," June 19, 1980: 18A

1443. "$1 Million Daily Is Spent at Fort," June 9, 1980: 1A

1444. "1,000 Troops, Police on Guard At Fort McCoy,"

September 10, 1980: 1A

1445. "Plan Angers Congressmen," June 21, 1980: 1A

1446. "Plans for Cubans Returning to Fort Cause Differences," October 1, 1980: 13A

1447. "Pledge to Repay States For Refugee Aid Falls Short of Expectations," July 14, 1980: 5A

1448. "Police Change Is 'Proceeding' At Fort Chaffee," December 16, 1980: 7A

1449. "Police Express Concern For Security at Chaffee, Riot Control Promised," August 6, 1980: 3A

1450. "Port to Stay Open, Cuban Quoted; Flotilla Battles Seas," April 26, 1980: 19A

1451. "Potential Sponsors Still Lacking For 4, 000 at Chaffee, Officials Say," July 9, 1980: 13A

1452. "President Orders End To Seaborne Influx Of Cuban Refugees," May 15, 1980: 1A

1453. "Problems Develop In Processing Cubans," May 11, 1980: 1A

1454. "Protection Sought For Cubans," August 1, 1980: p.1A

1455. "Psychiatric Clinic Opens at Chaffee To Treat Refugees," June 11, 1980: p. 5A

1456. "Puerto Rican Guard Called to Fort Chaffee; 30 Cubans Leave Camp," May 22, 1980: p. 13A

1457. "Reagan Attacks Carter on Cubans," October 31, 1980: p.3A

1458. "Refugee Airlift to Begin This Week If Clinton Endoreses Security Plan," September 24, 1980: p. 2A

1459. "Refugee Arrivals Exceed Estimates; 60,940 Reach U.S.," May 20, 1980: p. 1A

1460. "Refugee Center Avoiding Unrest That Hit Chaffee," June 8, 1980: p .1A

1461. "Refugee Flow Indicates Castro Has Rejected Carter Offer of Exodus," May 21, 1980: p. 3A

1462. "Refugee Halfway Houses Envisioned," November 8, 1980: p.5A

1463. "Refugee Leader at Fort Is Relieved of Duties," September 3, 1980: p.9A

1464. "Refugee, 16, Stabbed at Chaffee; Cuban Youth Is Arrested," November 14, 1980: p.10A

1465. "Refugees Captured; Security Is Criticized," May 28,

1980: p. 1A

1466. "Refugees Cleared In Mental Check Arrive at Chaffee," November 8, 1980: p.1A

1467. "Refugee's Ear Cut Off in Fight At Fort Chaffee," December 17, 1980: p.19A

1468. "Refugees Get Winter Clothes," October 27, 1980: p.3A

1469. "Refugees 'Scum' And Can't Return, Castro Paper Says," September 17, 1980: p.1A

1470. "Refugee Shot In Escape Try At Fort Chaffee," June 15, 1980: p. 4A

1471. "Refugees to Arrive In Arkansas Today; Fort Chaffee Readied," May 9, 1980: p. 1A

1472. "Refugees Won't Come to Chaffee Until October, Newspaper Reports," September 20, 1980: p.7A

1473. "Remaining Refugees Will Be Assigned To Fort Chaffee," August 2, 1980" p.1A

1474. "Residents Report Cubans In Area, Patrols Increase," September 5, 1980: p.3A

1475. "Responses by U.S. On Chaffee Issues Called Ambiguous," September 18, 1980: p.6A

1476. "Screening of Refugees Reveals Fourth Have Questionable Past," May 18, 1980: p. 1A

1477. "Sealift Toll Rises to 26," May 27, 1980: p. 1A

1478. "Seek Aid, Fort Smith Is Urged," May 14, 1980: p. 2A

1479. "78 at Chaffee Request Return to Cuba; Most Say They're Homesick," August 22, 1980: p. 6A

1480. "648 Cuban Refugees Arrive at Fort Chaffee," October 8, 1980: p.10A

1481. "16 Cubans Take Part In Uprising," June 20, 1980: p. 16A

1482. "60 Formerly at Chaffee Hold Protest," June 17, 1980: p. 5A

1483. "68 'Troublemakers' Are Isolated At Cuban Refugee Camp in Florida," May 29, 1980: p. 2A

1484. "Sociologist Finds Many Crimes Unreported at Fort Chaffee," September 10, 1980: p.3A

1485. "Soldier Takes 2 Cubans From Fort; All Arrested Near Oklahoma City," July 22, 1980: p. 9A

1486. "State Delegation, Local Officials Talk About Refugees," August 22, 1980: p.6A

1487. "Stockade Opened at Fort Chaffee as 5 Cubans Leave, 3 Held in Vehicle Thefts," May 23, 1980: :p .12A

1488. "10 Refugees Die As Ship Capsizes In Florida Straits," May 18, 1980: p. 1A

1489. "13 Arrested at Chaffee Following Disturbance," December 3. 1980: p.8A

1490. "37 Cubans Flown To Atlanta; Some Involved in Riot," June 12, 1980: p. 3A

1491. "Thousands Riot at Fort Chaffee, 15 Troopers, 4 Refugees Injured," June 2, 1980: p. 1A

1492. "Three Cubans Apprehened," June 15, 1980: p. 2A

1493. "3 Cubans Leave Chaffee, Apprehended at Barling," August 30, 1980: p.7A

1494. "3 Cubans Suspected As Agents," May 8, 1980: p. 3A

1495. "300 Cubans Block Chaffee Gate, Threaten to Go on Hunger Strike," May 31, 1980: p. 1A

1496. "300 Refugees To Be Released At Fort Chaffee," June 1, 1980: p. 1A

1497. "3 Officials Praise Clinton's Handling Of Cuba Refugees," October 29, 1980: p.4A

1498. "Three Refugees At Chaffee Hurt In 3 Assaults," November 18, 1980: p.9A

1499. "392 More Cubans From Fort McCoy Arrive at Chaffee," September 28, 1980: p.4A

1500. "35 Pct. Of Cubans May Be Deported, White House Says," May 14, 1980: p. 1A

1501. "Tide of Refugees Slackens in Florida; 868 Come Ashore," May 9, 1980: p. 1A

1502. "Town Pays Refugee's Return to Fort," November 23, 1980: p.4A

1503. "Top Officials Are Replaced After Fort Riot," June 19, 1980: p. 2A

1504. "Troop Cuts Worry Officials," December 6, 1980:p.1A

1505. "Troop Reduction at Chaffee 'Unacceptable,' Clinton Says; Delay, Limits Urged," December 4, 1980: p.8A

1506. "T-shirts Mark Riot at Chaffee," June 11, 1980: p. 2A

1507. "Two Cubans Are Stabbed At Fort Chaffee," October 2, 1980: p.13A

1508. "2 Cubans Indicted In Assault," June 26, 1980: p. 2A

1509. "2 Cubans Want to Return to Fort, Say They Weren't Fed at Ozark," July 17, 1980: p. 7A

1510. "2 Shrimp Boats Bring 42 Cubans to Florida; 37 From Peru Embassy," April 22, 1980: p. 1A

1511. "Two Sinking Vessels Filled With Refugees Sought; 215 on Board," April 28, 1980: p. 2A

1512. "295 Refugees Arrive At Chaffee From Eglin After Flight Diverted," September 26, 1980: p.2A

1513. "276 More Cubans Arrive; Barracks Heat Not Yet On," September 29, 1980:p.2A

1514. "$213,850 Is Owed For Refugee Care, Clinton Tells U.S.," June 26, 1980: p. 1A

1515. "21 Refugees Transferred to Atlanta," November 2, 1980:p.12A

1516. "U.S. May Jail Boat Captains In Cuba Sealift," May 16, 1980: p. 1A

1517. "U.S. Might Return 2,000 Cubans, Accept 25,000 More, Paper Says," January 16, 1981

1518. "U.S. to Close Havana Refugee Office," May 5, 1980: p. 1A

1519. "U.S. Vows Stiff Fines For Sealift,"April 24, 1980: p.1A

1520. "U.S. Will Let Most Cubans, Haitians Stay," June 21, 1980: p. 1A

1521. "Use Carrier, Clinton Says," May 14, 1980: p. 1A

1522. "Use of Fort Rest of '80 Is Asked," July 26, 1980: p.1A

1523. "Washington Link Speeds Interviews Of Cuba Refugees," May 14, 1980: p. 2A

1524. "Weep for Fidel? His Troubles Never End," April 17, 1980: p. 13A

1525. "White Attacks Carter Remarks On Fort Chaffee," October 11, 1980:p.7a

1526. "White Promises He Will 'Stand Up' To U.S. on Cubans," January 19, 1981

1527. "White to Seek Move of Cubans," December 5, 1980: p.1A

1528. "Will Arrest Cubans, Community Officials Near Chaffee Warn," May 29, 1980: p. 1A

1527. "Workers at Chaffee Allege Jobs Being Lost, Arkansans Replaced," October 24, 1980: p.7A

Chronology
of the
Mariel Boatlift
March-November 1980

March 28

A bus with over 30 Cubans seeking political asylum crashes into the Peruvian Embassy. A Cuban guard is killed in the cross-fire.

April 4

Cuban guards posted outside the Peruvian Embassy withdrawn in reaction to death of a guard shot during an attempt by Cubans to crash into the Embassy compound.

April 4

The Government of Cuba withdraws police protection around the Peruvian Embassy announcing that anyone wishing to leave should go to the Embassy. Over 10,000 Cubans seek asylum in less than 48 hours.

April 6

Responding to the announcement by GOC, 10,800 Cubans jam into Embassy in the two days since the announcement.

April 8

Cuban Refugees at the Peruvian Embassy send messages to President Carter, Pope Paul II and other Heads of State requesting assistance in leaving Cuba.

April 10

Goverment of Perú calls for urgent measures to assist with international resettlement of 10,000 Cubans gathered in Peruvian Embassy in Havana.

April 11

United States announces military exercises to be carried out in the US and the naval base at Guantánamo.

April 14-18

Flights from Havana to Costa Rica carried some 1,000 refugees, about half of whom were subsequently taken to Perú.

April 14

President signs determination to admit up to 3,500 Cuban refugees from Peruvian Embassy and to fund transportation and other costs through a $4.25 million-drawn down from Emergency Refugee & Migration Fund.

April 15

Anti-U.S. demonstrations are staged in Havana two blocks from the U.S. Interest Section. "Yankee Go Home" slogans are shouted.

United Nations General Waldheim asks the UNHCR to be ready to provide assistance in Costa Rica or in any other country the Cubans seek to go.

April 16

A U.S. licensed aircraft airlifts 150 Cuban refugees at the Peruvian Embassy from Cuba to Costa Rica in the first flight to leave Cuba. The refugees are met in San José by Costa Rican President Carazo.

An estimated 7,488 refugees leave Cuba. 500 to Spain, 420 to Costa Rica and 368 to Perú. Of the 6,200 going to the United States, an estimated one-fourth were not at the Peruvian Embassy in Havana.

April 18

Castro suspended the airlift declaring that henceforth only refugee flights to countries of final destination would be permitted.

On the 19th anniversary of the Bay of Pigs invasion, hundreds of thousands of signs carrying Cubans march past the Peruvian Embassy to show support for Castro.

April 19

Anti-Castro demonstrators march at the UN in New York to show support for their compatriots at the Peruvian Embassy in Havana.

The Costa Rican Foreign Ministry sends a message to Castro saying it is willing to grant permanent asylum to "all" 10,000 Cubans. The message also appeals for the resumption of evacuation flights.

Two privately owned US boats sail into the Cuban port of Mariel and pick up 49 Cuban refugees from the Peruvian Embassy. The boats are the first of a flotilla that will transport Cuban refugees to the U.S.

April 20

Castro regime announced that all Cuban wishing to emigrate to the U.S. were free to board boats at the port of Mariel.

April 21

"Freedom Flotilla" began. Within hours of Castro's April 20 announcement, Cuban-Americans were on their way to Cuba to pick up relatives.

April 29

The Federal Emergency Management Agency (FEMA) established a coordination team in Miami to deal with the crisis.

The U.S. cancels the military exercises that were scheduled to take place at Guantánamo in May. The ships that were to take part in the exercise will now aid the refugee flotilla.

May 1 - May 31
Total Cuban arrivals 94,181.

May 2
Violence breaks out at, the US Interest Section in Havana when a pro-Castro mob attacks a group of Cubans seeking exit visas to leave Cuba. About 400 individuals take refuge in USINT.

INS intensifies screening at Key West to ascertain whether arrivals have immediate family in South Florida. If so, send to Miami if not, send to Eglin.

White House announced that President Carter has authorized spending $10 million for processing Cuban/Haitian: "boat people" at Eglin, money coming from Refugee Emergency Fund and will constitute initial costs of starting processing facility.

May 3
Cuban newspaper accuses USINT personnel of provoking the violent incident of May 2.

Eglin Air Force Base, Florida opens as a reception center.

President Carter tells the League of Women Voters in Philadelphia that they (Cubans) would be welcomed with "an open heart and open arms."

May 5
Health and Human Sciences offered staff assistance to the State Department in coordinating voluntary resettlement agencies who are assisting Cubans. No financial resources may be appropriated from Refugee appropriations.

May 6
U.S. Department of Agriculture decides Cubans are eligible for food stamps if they are registered to work.

President Carter declared a state of emergency for South Florida and approved the use of $10 million in refugee emergency found to reimburse voluntary organizations for their overhead expenses at processing centers and for costs of transporting the Cuban exiles from the centers to their final destinations.

May 7
FEMA assigns the mission to U.S. Army to provide appropriate military personnel, resources and equipment for the purpose of supporting the total Federal efforts associated with the reception, processing and resettlement of refugees in Florida and other areas in the United States.

White House notifies Rep. John Paul Hammerschmidt that an undetermined number of refugees will be sent to Ft. Chaffee Army Reserve base for processing to reportedly begin within 10 days.

The U.S. press reports at least 20 Cuban intelligence agents have been identified among the Cuban refugees entering Florida on the boat lift.

Havana domestic radio criticizes Costa Rica for holding an international meeting on the refugee problem; the broadcast affirms that the issue is between the US and Cuba only.

400 US Marines are dispatched to Key West to help maintain order and provide logistical assistance in the processing of the Cuban refugees.

May 8

Fort Chaffee, Arkansas opens as a reception center.

May 8-9

San José Conference of 22 countries and 7 international organizations where at least ten countries pledged to accept Cubans for permanent resettlement. Several others offered financial aid to either the Intergovernmental Committee on European Migration (ICEM) or the United Nations High Commissioner for Refugees.

May 9

Eglin AFB reception center filled to capacity (9,700 persons)

May 10

Opalaka becomes operational.

May 13

FEMA decides to transfer all unaccompanied minors to Fort Chaffee (including those who have relatives in South Florida.)

A White House spokesman says that 35% of the arriving Cuban refugees who have no US relatives may not be allowed to remain. He adds that the US will rely on other countries to help with resettlement.

May 14

President Carter proposes an official US sealift and airlift of Cuban refugees with careful screening of those wishing to enter the US.

President Carter's statement
calling for a halt to "Freedom Flotilla"
offering a government run air & sea lift
instructing Coast Guard to stop boats going to Cuba.
making it illegal to do so.

May 17

An estimated one million Cubans march past the US Interest Section as the focal point of an island-wide series of anti-US demonstrations.

Fort Indiantown Gap, Pennsylvania opens as a reception center.

May 19
A US Coast Guard blockade is established to prevent boats from traveling to Cuba to take out refugees.

Cuba responds to President Carter's proposal for an orderly flow of refugees by insisting that U.S.-Cuban talks must cover all bilateral issues.

Fort Chaffee filled to capacity (18,972 persons).

May 22
Cuba rejects an offer by the US, Great Britian, and Costa Rica to negotiate an international solution to the Cuban refugee problem.

May 24
A Cuban patrol boat harasses a US Coast Guard vessel in international waters near the Cuban coast forcing it to take avoidance measures.

Hundreds of frustrated Cubans riot at Eglin some climb fences. Some are injured, none seriously.

May 29
Fort Indiantown Gap is filled to capacity (18,311 persons)
Fort McCoy, Wisconsin opens as a reception center.

June 1 B 30
Total Cuban Arrivals = 115,436.

June 1
Some 1000 Cubans riot at Ft. Chaffee. Two buildings are burned. State troopers and tear gas are needed to disperse the crowd. 84 Cubans are jailed.

June 2
Havana Domestic Service reports that a thousand Cubans, angry over delays in their resettlement, battle state and military police at the Ft. Chaffee relocation center; 45 people are injured and several buildings are destroyed by fire.

June 5
Havana announces that 33 Cuban refugees, who for various reasons have not been authorized to leave Cuba, remain at Peruvian Embassy. Havana states they must remain there or surrender to authorities.

Foreign Aid Authorization bill for FY'81 passes House with Fascell floor amendment. Amendment triggers the $100 million appropriated in Supplemental Appropriations Act for FY'80

Reimburses States up to 100% for cash and medical assistance and Social Services to Cuban/Haitian Entrants.

Permits President to direct executive agencies to provide processing and resettlement assistance for Cuban/Haitian Entrants.

Provides authorizing language for the $65 million "budget" amendment appropriation.

June 7

US gives the Government of Cuba a note protesting in the strongest possible terms the cynical actions of the GOC in sending to the United States hardened criminals who constitute a danger to any society "and requesting that Cuba accept the return of these persons."

June 9

As of May 31, FEMA reports $55.7 million in reimbursable costs had been expended or obligated by various Federal agencies.

June 11

Coast Guard reports first judicial hearing from improper operation or use of vessels during the Cuba to Key West sealift was held during the Operator charged-operating beyond scope of his license.

B improperly engaging in international voyage.

June 16

Fort McCoy is filled to capacity (13,258 persons)

June 17

Foreign Aid Authorization bill for FY'81 passes Senate with Stone floor amendment. Same as Fascell amendment.

June 30

Second San José Conference to discuss the humanitarian aspects of the Cuban-Haitian influx and the need for international cooperation particularly on the issue of mutual respect for immigration laws of the countries concerned.

July 1 B July 31

Total Cuban Arrivals = 118,065

July 2

US hands the Cuban Government a list of 65 Cubans citizens who arrived via Mariel and wished to return to Cuba. U.S. asked that the Cuban Interest Section make the necessary arrangements for their return to Cuba.

July 14

State Department temporarily withdraws 17 U.S. diplomats and dependents because of a "virulent and continuing anti-American campaign" in an effort to "pare down" the staff.

July 15

Cuba-Haitian Task Force assumes responsibility for camp operations from the Federal Emergency Management Agency (FEMA).

July 31

Cuban-Haitian Entrant Act of 1980 submitted to Congress by the Administration.

Creates special Cuban-Haitian entrant status.

Defines services and benefits for arrivals

Specifies criteria for federal reimbursement to States.

August 1 B 31

Total Cuban Arrivals = 121,994

August 5

Senator Kennedy introduces the Cuban/Haitian Entrant Act of 1980 (S. 3013)

Created special Cuban-Haitian entrant status

Defines services and benefits for arrivals

Specifies criteria for federal reimbursement to States.

Kennedy introduces Amendment No. 1962 to S. 3013

Declares Cubans Haitians defined by Administration's bill to be refugees eligible for benefit provisions of Refugee Act of 1980.

Provides federal reimbursement at levels specified in Act 100%.

A series of disturbances involving several hundred Cubans brakes out at Ft. Indiantown Gap. The 82nd Air Borne is called in to tighten security. About 70 Cubans are moved into the Louisberg prison.

President Carter signs Presidential Determination to increase the amount of ERMA funds available to $20 million and States that the money is to be used for those Cubans and Haitians applying for "political asylum".

August 17

US presents a note to the GOC pointing out that "it has long been recognized as a matter of customary international law that a State has a duty to receive back its own nationals", and proposing conversations on an urgent basis to provide a mechanism for the identification and repatriation.

Sept. 1 B 30

Total Cuban Arrivals = 125,262

Sept. 25

288 Cubans are flown to Ft. Chaffee from the reception center at Eglin Air Force Base. This begins consolidation at Chaffee.

Sept. 26

Castro closes Mariel and orders all boats awaiting passengers to leave. 125,262 Cubans have arrived at Key West via Mariel.

Last flights from Eglin to Chaffee carry 327 Cubans. Ft. McCoy enters consolidation process sending 117 to Ft. Chaffee.

Sept. 27

394 Cubans arrive in Ft. Chaffee from Ft. McCoy.

Sept. 28

268 Cubans arrive in Ft. Chaffee from Ft. McCoy.

November 19

First of 600 Cuban refugees, stranded in Mariel when Boatlift ended, begin arriving by air in Miami.